Learning

Accelerated Learning and Speed Reading Guide to Learn, Memorize and Read Faster and Learn Languages Like Spanish, French Quickly

(Better Memory and Study Skills)

Josh Dryden

Published by Rob Miles

© **Josh Dryden**

All Rights Reserved

Memory Improvement: Accelerated Learning and Speed Reading Guide to Learn, Memorize and Read Faster and Learn Languages Like Spanish, French Quickly (Better Memory and Study Skills)

ISBN 978-1-7771171-3-9

Legal & Disclaimer

The information contained in this book is not designed to replace or take the place of any form of medicine or professional medical advice. The information in this book has been provided for educational and entertainment purposes only.

The information contained in this book has been compiled from sources deemed reliable, and it is accurate to the best of the Author's knowledge; however, the Author cannot guarantee its accuracy and validity and cannot be held liable for any errors or omissions. Changes are periodically made to this book. You must consult your doctor or get professional medical advice before using any of the suggested remedies, techniques, or information in this book.

Table of Contents

Introduction

Let's start with a quick pop quiz...

1. Which light comes on top of the traffic signal - red or green?

2. Can you name the planets in our solar system?

3. Without looking, answer this question: is the number 6 on the dial of your watch the Roman numeral VI or the number '6'?

4. What is Newton's third law of motion?

Don't know? Can't remember? Don't worry – you're not alone.

Not all of us can be Einstein or Leonardo da Vinci. And that's quite alright.

Great thinkers who have interpreted the marvels of the world for us are people with impressive learning skills and amazing memories. Granted, few amongst us can ever have that kind of influence on society. All the same, your career, your hobby or your interests may require you to learn something new, well after you've left your college corridors. Your quest for knowledge and self improvement can play a very important part in your life, leading you to greater successes, better job prospects and fantastic pay packages.

It has been said that each one of us makes use of only 12% of our learning and retention capabilities. There are a number of reasons for this: partly, it is because of the way we have been _{programmed} to learn and remember. All our study techniques are geared towards learning _{by rote} pages and pages of printed material – the hard way. This kind of learning uses only one part of the brain. So, we _{can} only ever make use of a limited portion of our brain.

This type of study is tedious and boring. It is also very time consuming.

When the world around you is changing rapidly and you need to keep up with its fast pace, finding time for training or extra study can itself be difficult. Poring over large textbooks and training material after a hectic day at the office and mugging it all up into the wee hours of the morning is not exactly exciting. Nor is it very productive.

Nevertheless, people still continue to do it.

Did you know?

• 96% of what most companies spend on development and training is a waste of money.

• 97% of companies use lecture and presentation as their primary method of instruction.

• In the absence of any coaching or follow-up instructions (as is the case in most company-assisted training programs), people remember only 22% of what they hear.

• Within 30 days of any training program, employees forget more than 80% of what they have learned.

The bottom line is: most people retain only 4% of what they hear and learn.

Surveys and research show one important thing:

• While companies are spending millions of dollars on training, employees are getting little or no benefits.

To be sure, companies are offering quality training courses and their employees are equally sincere in their efforts to learn.

Then what could be the rationale behind these awful figures?

Life-changing knowledge (the kind of knowledge that can bring you true results) requires learning techniques that help you learn quickly and retain everything you have learnt.

Accelerated learning techniques have been around for more than a century now, but they are still quite strange to us. Even today, a majority of students know little about accelerated learning techniques. They are still learning through memorizing what's in their books.

One reason for their anonymity is that these techniques are not followed within school rooms. Probably, teachers believe that these easy and fun methods of learning would detract from the seriousness of the subject in hand. In any case, practitioners of formal training and learning courses are afraid to experiment. Little wonder then that we are still stuck in the 18th and 19th centuries when it comes to learning and memorizing.

Imagine if you could learn and remember all the various things - regardless of whether it is your grocery list or hundreds of acts and laws from a fat textbook - in less than half the time it would take you ordinarily! And what if you had a method of learning that would store all the important data permanently in your brain? You could then recall this data - without any mistake - a week, month or two years from now.

If the very thought of speed learning and near-accurate retention is enough to get your adrenalin flowing, let's plunge straight ahead and take the super express highway towards rapid learning and sharp memorizing.

Chapter 1: How to Improve Your Memory

If you want to increase your memory, there are several things you can do right now, from eating blueberries to using a mixed bag of reminder tricks. If you're confident in yourself, you'll have the ability to increase your memory right away!

Trying Memory Tricks

Say things you need to remember out loud. If you experience trouble remembering whether you took your medicine each morning, simply say, "I just took my medicine!" right after you took it, to strengthen this thought in your brain. Saying this out loud will help you remember that you did take your medicine. This also lives up to expectations if you're meeting another individual and would prefer not to overlook his name. Simply repeat the name actually after you learn it: "Hello there, Sarah, it's nice to meet you." This also tries to remember a place or a meeting time. Simply repeat out loud to the individual who invited you: "The Grand Tavern at 7? That sounds great."

Improve your breathing when you need to remember something. When it's an ideal chance to study or remember something new, switch your breathing to be slower and deeper. Deeper and slower breathing surely changes the way your brain lives up to expectations, by making the brain's electrical heartbeats change to Theta waves, which regularly happens in your brain in hypnogogic rest.

Keep in mind a man's name. Use a famous trick out of FDR's playbook for remembering a man's name. At the point when a man accustoms themselves with you, picture them with their name composed on their brow. This will tell the picture of that individual with their name.

Squeeze an anxiety ball. Crushing an anxiety ball or making a clenched hand with your hand can help you remember a bit of data later. Before remembering the data, squeeze the anxiety ball in your prevailing hand. For a normal individual, this would be your right hand. When you have to recall the data, squeeze the anxiety ball in your inverse hand for no less than 45 seconds. This simple action may be sufficient to help you remember.

Chew gum. This basic revelation can strengthen the brain and increase your obsession, particularly if you have to remember data for 30 minutes or more. According to British Psychological Society (BPS) visual and sound-related memory increases when a man chews gum by keeping the individual more involved. When you have to recollect something for under 30 minutes, however, it is suggested not to chew on anything.

Move your eyes from side to side. Christman's research exposes that moving your eyes from side to side for only 30 seconds once every day will adjust the two sections of your brain and make your memory work all the more easily. Attempt this life hack when you wake up in the morning.

Smell rosemary. Prof Mark Moss at Northumbria University reveals that noticing rosemary can improve your memories. Bring a sprig of rosemary or smell rosemary oil once every day. The Ancient Greeks even put a sprig of rosemary behind their ears on exam days to help them increase their memories.

Using Mindful Approaches

Quit believing that you have an "awful memory." We all have them - those hateful recollections that make us want to creep under the bed to avoid the past. Terrible recollections can turn into all-devouring if you don't address the issue head on. Facing the recollections and portraying them out loud is a compelling tactic to defuse the tension they bring. It may need some investment, however, if you're resolved to preventing the memories from filling up your brain, you'll find the courage to talk about them. Delete those considerations and promise yourself to increase your memory's capacity. Commend even little accomplishments to keep yourself inspired.

Exercise your brain. Regularly "working out" the brain keeps it capacity increasing and goals the advancement of new nerve associations that can help increase memory. By increasing new mental abilities - particularly complex ones, for example, taking in another language or figuring out how to play another musical instrument - and testing your brain with puzzles and recreations, you can keep your brain active and improve its physiological working. Try some ordinary, fun puzzle practices, for example, crosswords, Sudoku, and different diversions which are sufficiently simple for anybody. Get out of your normal range of familiarity and pick something that is new and testing, which makes you flex your brain strengths. Attempt to play chess or a quick paced table game. A vast part of your brain is initiated when it takes in another aptitude. Adapting new data is also useful, yet since aptitudes require both the admission and yield of data, they practice a bigger bit of your brain.

Give yourself a chance to enclose a memory. Memories are extremely elusive in the short-term, and diversions can make you rapidly overlook something as basic as a telephone number. The way to refrain from losing recollections before you can even frame them is to have the ability to focus on the thing to be associated with for a while without contemplating on different things, so when you're trying to remember something, maintain a strategic distance from diversions and convoluted assignments for a couple of minutes.

Improving Your Lifestyle

Using Mnemonic Devices

Use associations to remember actualities. A mnemonic is something which can be used to recall things much less demanding. As is regularly the case, it could be an expression, a short melody, or something that is well recalled, that we use to recollect something else that would somehow be difficult to remember. To use associations successfully, you can make a picture in your psyche to help you remember a word or a picture. For example, if you experience serious difficulties remembering JFK was the president involved in the Bay of Pigs attack, simply picture the President swimming in a sea included by cheerful, oinking pigs. This is completely senseless, however, this solid picture in your brain will perpetually help you connect the president with this event.

Use associations to remember numbers. Suppose you continue overlooking your understudy ID each time you have to use it. Simply separate the number into littler lumps and make pictures connected with those pieces. Suppose the number is 12-7575-23. Figure out how to make these numbers important. Suppose "12" happens to be your home number, "75" happens to be your grandma's age, and the number "23" is Michael Jordan's shirt number. This is what you can imagine recalling the number:

Use piecing. Chunking breaks a wide rundown of numbers or different sorts of data into smaller, more reasonable pieces. Breaking so as to recall a 10-digit telephone number it down into three arrangements of numbers: 555-867-5309.

Use poems and similar sounding word usage. Poems, similar sounding word usage, and even jokes are a supreme approach to recall more everyday statistical data points. Using a mixture of regular and senseless rhymes can help you review fundamental data. For example, if you're attempting to make sense of if April has 30 or 31 days, simply say the old rhyme out loud: "Thirty days has September, April, June, and November." Then you'll recollect that April does, in reality, have 30 days. Here are some different rhymes to use as memory tools: In 1492, Columbus sailed the sea blue. A child can take in the letter set by singing it to the tune of Twinkle, Twinkle, and Little Star, which makes the letters poem.

Using acronyms. Acronyms are another excellent tool for recollecting a mixture of things, from the names of the five Great Lakes to the words used as conjunctions. You can apply a prominent acronym, or make one for yourself. For instance, if you're setting off to the store and know you just need Butter, Lettuce, Bread, and Uncage, then simply make a word out of the first letter of every term: BULB - Butter, Uncage, Lettuce, and Bread. Here are some prominent acronyms to utilize:

HOMES. This one is used for remembering the Great Lakes: Huron, Ontario, Michigan, Erie, and Superior.

ROY G. BIV. This man's name can aid you to recall the shades of the rainbow: Red, Orange, Yellow, Green, Blue, Indigo, and Violet.

FOIL. This will aid you to remember how to increase two binomial terms: First, Outer, Inner, Last.

FANBOYS. This acronym can aid you to remember straightforward organizing conjunctions: For, And, Nor, But, Or, Yet, So.

Use puzzles. Puzzles are like acronyms, with the exception of rather than simply recollecting the acronym, you can recall another sentence made out of the first letters of an arrangement of words that you need to retain in a sure request. For instance, you can say, "My very enthusiastic mother – Jane - sent us noodles." to remember the order of the planets: Mercury, Venus, Earth, Mars, Jupiter, Saturn, Uranus, and Neptune. You can also make up acrostics of your claim. Here are a couple of more prominent puzzles: Each Good Boy Does Good. This is used for retaining the lines on the treble music staff: EGBDF. Never Eat Sour Watermelons. This is used for remembering the purposes of a compass in the clockwise request: North, East, South, and West. Another great sample is Never Eat Shredded Wheat which also rhymes too. Ruler Philip Can Only Find His Green Slippers. Use this to remember the request of the classification framework: Kingdom, Phylum, Class, Order, Family, Genus, and Species. Please Excuse My Dear Aunt Sally. Utilize this to recall the request of operations in science: Parenthesis, Exponents, Multiplication, Division, Addition, and Subtraction.

Use the method of loci. This method has been used since the times of Ancient Greece. This process obliges you to partner things as far as an area to help you remember the full plan of data. To use this technique, just envision putting the things you need to recall along with a course you're very acquainted with, or in specific areas in a well-known room or building. To start off, imagine your walk to the store; then, picture the things you need to do or recall along that way.

CHAPTER 2:The Most Important Benefits

of Speed Reading

Why would you spend your precious time learning how to read faster? Well, there are a lot of reasons why. First of all, finishing two books within five hours is much better and much more productive than finishing just one book. Many people often make the wrong assumption that speed reading is just about reading quicker. There are a lot of benefits of speed reading that you might not be aware of. Let's take a closer look into some of the more important benefits of speed reading. These should convince you that speed reading has much more to offer than just the skill of being able to read more words in less time.

Speed reading enables you to read faster. Well, this is a no-brainer. This is in fact the number one reason why people try to learn speed reading in the first place. Let's take this book that you are reading for example. This book contains around 8,000 words. For an average reader, it may take him three to five hours to finish reading the book. But if you are skilled in the art of speed reading, you can finish this whole book in just two hours or less. In a nutshell, speed reading improves your productivity as well as your consumption of textual content. You have the ability to read and understand more words in much less time.

Speed reading allows you to absorb information much faster. As you learn how to skim through words, sentences, and paragraphs, you are also training yourself to understand what they mean quicker. You can look at a paragraph, speed read through it, and process the information at the same time. It is easier to absorb the information because your eyes and brain have been conditioned to take them in faster.

Speed reading improves your overall comprehension skills. Comprehension is your ability to make sense of what you are reading. Being able to read faster doesn't amount to anything if you fail to understand what you are reading. Speed reading isn't just about reading quicker, it's also about comprehending what you are reading. The two come hand in hand. Without an improvement in comprehension skills, speed reading is useless.

Speed reading promotes visualization while reading. It's no secret that it's easier to understand what you are reading if you can visualize it in your mind. When you speed read, your eyes and brain go on overdrive. They become more active, more alert. With that said, your visualization capabilities are also heightened. Your brain learns how to paint pictures much faster than usual.

Speed reading offers strategies that can help you deal with today's information overload. This is without a doubt one of the major reasons why speed reading is becoming more popular these days. More people are looking for ways on how to organize and screen the barrage of information that they get every single day.

For instance, when you log into your Facebook account, your newsfeed will be overflowing with tons of information. How do you quickly browse through your newsfeed and separate the valuable ones from the useless ones? Speed reading can help you in this scenario. Speed reading helps you focus on the pieces of information that matter and disregard all the rest.

Speed reading helps you in getting rid of bad reading habits that you may have developed from school or from your childhood. For example, many people can't seem to read without moving their lips or mouthing the words. This is a bad reading habit that slows down both your reading and comprehension skills. With proper speed reading exercises, you can slowly but efficiently break down this bad habit.

Speed reading promotes concentration and discipline. The skill requires you to focus on the task ahead and that is to read the text as quickly as you can. The more you do this, the better your concentration becomes. It also breeds discipline. You will learn how to build a barrier against outside influence and just focus on reading.

Speed reading encourages you to learn memory techniques. Memory retention is closely affiliated with speed reading. Remember that speed reading is about reading quicker without losing your ability to understand the text that you are poring through. As you read faster, you are also conditioning your brain to become better in memorizing things. In other words, speed reading plays a significant role in improving your memory retention capabilities.

Speed reading allows you to decide faster what is worth reading and what's not. Again, this is very important these days wherein you are regularly bombarded with tons of content whether online or offline. With speed reading, it will take you less time to sort out what you should read and what you should ignore. Let's say for instance that you get several emails every single day. With speed reading, you can quickly browse through your inbox and determine which messages are urgent and which messages should go straight to the trash bin.

Speed reading can help you develop a more efficient and clearer writing style. You may be wondering about the possible connection between speed reading and writing styles. Well, if you are a good speed reader, you tend to be more economical when you write. This is because your brain has been conditioned to read more efficiently. So when you write, you are also focused in writing more efficiently. This means that your writing style will be more concise and more direct to the point.

Speed reading opens up more time for you to spend on other activities that you may be interested in. Look, if you can read a book in one hour instead of two hours, that means you will have an extra free hour to do other things. In a way, speed reading is somewhat similar to a time management tool. It helps you get things done quicker so that you can have more time to perform other tasks. If you are a student, this means you will have more time to engage in extracurricular activities. If you are an office secretary, this can possibly mean you can go home earlier. If you are a teacher, you can finish your lesson plans in half the time you usually need to get things done. And so on and so forth.

As you can see, speed reading is much more than just the ability to read faster. It offers a ton of benefits that can make your life easier. The great thing about speed reading is that you can easily get started learning it anytime. Just grab the book nearest to you and start practicing using any of the techniques discussed in this book. You can dive right into Chapter Four of this book to take a quick glance of these speed reading techniques and exercises. You can practice speed reading anywhere. At the subway, on your way to work, at the park while sitting at a bench, at home while sipping through a cup of coffee, or maybe on your nightly reading before you go to sleep.

CHAPTER 3: The nature of memory

Is human memory really unlimited?

Scientific research into this subject indicates that the memory capacity of the average human brain is of an order of magnitude greater than was previously thought. According to one study, our estimated memory capacity has increased, by a conservative estimate, by a factor of 10 to at least one petabyte. In other words, the human brain may be able to store an astonishing 1,000,000,000,000,000 bytes of information. That is enough memory capacity to store, for instance, 13.3 years of high-definition video. Google processes over 20 petabytes of data every day, whilst Facebook (at the last count) had some 60 billion images, which equals 1.5 petabytes of storage.

Such studies into the brain's natural storage capacity constitute an important advance in our understanding of human neuroanatomy and could be a step closer to the creation of a complete "wiring diagram" of the human brain. Since the brain contains several billion neural synapses, researchers now believe that their calculations point to truly amazing levels of human brain processing power. There is no doubt that, considered in terms of the normal everyday usages to which we need to put our memory storage abilities, the human memory is to all intents and purposes practically unlimited.

Why, then, do people want to improve their memory?

Well, at the most "human" level, our memory is so important to us that we often say in ordinary parlance that "a person does not die so long as he or she is remembered by others". So memory can make us immortal in the eyes of others, if you will. Memory is also important in the race by medical researchers to find a cure for the disease known as Alzheimer's, which—by robbing individuals of their short-term and long-term memories—effectively leaves them dehumanized, a mere shell compared to the lively and vital person they once were. The above are just two instances in which memory is fundamental to our sense of self-identity. This is similarly the case when we remember memories of childhood, which contribute to helping us understand the family and social context that we came from as individuals. Happy childhood memories, for examples, are apt to last a lifetime and become something to treasure during the adult phase of life. However, memory has also shown itself to be highly selective, with the ability to repress negative memories which have accumulated during one's life in the interests of "good mental hygiene".

Memories come to us with such force and vitality sometimes that they cannot be eradicated in the normal course of events. The memory of someone you have deeply loved, for example, remains with you all throughout your life. This contributes to the emotional pain and sense of loss that we feel when we are bereaved. Memories of this strength cannot be erased with any machine known to man. But most important of all, memory in middle and old age becomes a repository of all the experience and distilled wisdom that the person has accumulated up to that point. By reflecting on past experiences in relation to the present circumstances of our lives, we are able to avoid stumbling into the same habitual errors and mistakes that we have made before.

In our current society, which is characterized by constant movement and ever higher levels of pressure, "vagueness of memory" is something that can easily be addressed and corrected, thus leaving us better equipped to deal with the huge demands placed on us by our everyday lives. Having digital agendas and to-do lists, placing sticky notes around the house and Googling for the information you need at your fingertips sometimes does the trick, but there is no replacement for an optimally functioning biological memory. In fact, people with superb memory are slowly becoming the exception rather than the norm today since we use so many electronic aids and devices as memory

Chapter 4: Improving Your Memory

Once you start to become more effective at picking up new information then you might start to wonder just exactly how you are going to keep track of everything in your head. It's extremely important to learn some new organizational skills and some strategies of making sure that your memory can be able to keep up with everything that you are trying to accomplish.

After all, what good is new knowledge attained if you can't remember it long enough to make it useful for you? Let's take a look at some great ways to train yourself to remember more and make a real difference in the way that you approach everyday situations.

Use Associations

In order to make things stick in your mind, you need to make sure that you find connections that you can relate to. Try using word associations to understand your information more clearly and to remember it easier. In addition, if you can connect to the new information by using a strange or unique association in your mind, then you are even more likely to hang on to it with ease.

Chunk Things Together

Organization is important when it comes to remembering new facts. Try putting the information that you are going over into smaller groups so that it's easier for you to retain. For example break a long string of numbers into groups of 4 or 5 instead. It's the same way that we do phone numbers or social security numbers so you are subconsciously accustomed to doing this anyway. Don't try to overwhelm yourself with information. Learning smaller pieces first, on there on, then stringing them together can be much more effective!

Try Rhyming

There is a reason why children's songs and books are put into rhyming forms; it makes them easier to remember and repeat back. You can use this method as an adult as well and it will go a long way towards helping you to remember a whole host of information. Think about the rhyme that you might have heard regarding the number of days in a month. "30 days has September, April, June and November." Because it rhymes, it easily rolls off of the tongue and helps keeps the information in your mind for later use. This makes it easier to recall whenever you need to pull it back up again.

Acronyms Can Help

With certain lists or types of material, you can't rhyme them or break them down any further. However, with these types of things you can sometimes find a way to turn them into an acronym for easier retention. One example of this is a pretty common one for schoolchildren. Think of the colors of the rainbow' and easier way to remember them in the correct order is to think of the name ROY G. BIV. Red, orange, yellow, green, blue, indigo and violet are names that can be a lot harder to keep in mind then the short simple acronym.

Try Using an Acrostic

Another little memory trick that can be useful for you to learn is making an acrostic with the information that you want to remember. This is similar to an acronym; however instead of making a new word, you make a sentence with the first letters of the words. Take for example, the directions on the compass, North, East, South and West. You can remember these easier with an acrostic like, "Never eat soggy worms." The key is to make things unique or off kilter a bit so that they stick out in your mind.

CHAPTER 5: OVER THE PHONE

INTERVIEWS

An over the phone interview is not less valuable than an interview performed face to face. In today's society taking time to meet with every probable candidate can make the interviewing process take longer and keep companies from filling much needed positions. Many companies have moved their interview process to be compiled of a phone interview followed by a face to face interview. This allows them to move through candidates more quickly but meet with more of them for a more thorough search for the best candidate.

While a face to face interview allows you to use your body language and be charismatic in person, this does not mean a phone interview won't allow you the same opportunities. With an over the phone interview often perspective employers are checking on the swiftness and thoroughness of your responses as well as your punctuality and organizational abilities. If you spend a lot of time searching for answers to questions this will signal the interviewer that you may not be as organized, or even qualified for the position as they thought. This of course is depending on the type of work.

A good and well written resume is no longer enough to gain you interest as a candidate. Telephone interviews are good ways to weed out candidates who are not fully serious about the position, are under qualified, or simply not a good fit. These initial interviews are screening interviews which allow companies to narrow down their candidate search.

From this short list of candidates they are able to narrow down the search to a handful of people whom they would like to meet in person. This is not always the case as there are times a phone interview is the only interview and you could be offered a position without meeting face to face. Again each company and even each supervisor will run their interview process differently.

There are times when a supervisor may call and create what is called an **unscheduled interview.** These types of impromptu calls never work in your favor and it is best to reschedule the call at a time when you have the ability to be prepared and be in a quiet space. Be polite and express that you are unable to give the call the attention it deserves at the moment and would like to schedule a time when it would be beneficial for both parties. If they are truly interested in you as a candidate they will be willing to schedule an interview.

Scheduled phone interviews will often make their first contact with you through e-mail or by phone and will request a time in which you will be able to speak. In that time you will be able to prepare yourself for your discussion and present yourself to the best of your ability. The goal is to turn a phone interview into a job offer or face to face meeting.

When taking part in a phone interview it is best to still dress the part. The feeling of professionalism will carry through weather you are in person or not. Wearing your pajamas to your phone interview may make you behave in too casual a manner but dressing as though you are attending the interview in person puts you in a similar mindset as though your were meeting your interviewer face to face.

Furthermore, be sure to have a quite and calm place to conduct your conversation. Having a phone interview with background noise can be distracting not only for you but the other person on the line. Interviewing can be especially nerve wracking so having a place which is calm will help you collect your answers with composure.

Keeping a copy of your resume with you will help you refer to the document should your interviewer have questions. Being able to look to your document will allow you to answer more quickly and not allow nerves to rule over your conversation. Consider your resume as your safety blanket because we all have black outs in our thoughts when under pressure or extreme amounts of stress.

Go to your selected place for your interview ten to fifteen minutes early. Get comfortable and allow yourself to be at ease before beginning the call. If you are using a cell phone be sure to have your phone charged and the charger nearby. A notepad to take notes as you are on the phone will allow you to look back over the conversation and ask any questions you may have if given the opportunity.

Ensure you are able to answer the call when it comes in as there are times when companies simply will not provide another opportunity to interview if your windowed time slot is not met. Conducting phone interviews provides companies a larger range of people they can consider as they are more convenient and can take less time in the day. If your window of opportunity is missed the chance is high there will not be an opportunity to make up the interview. This is why being prepared and early to your chosen space is important and gives less chance of missing your interview.

In a phone interview it is a good idea to listen first. This eliminates a risk of talking over your interviewer. This also allows your interviewer a chance to set the expectations of the interview and be the leader. Take notes if you can while listening so that if any questions arise you will be able to refer back to your notes and be thorough in your discussion. Look for ways in which you can make connections. As the interviewer discusses the job you can connect similarities to the job you currently have or ones you have had in the past. Be sure to only speak when a pause is evident or you are asked a question.

Be sure that you are not dry in the mouth as you are unable to make a first impression with your physical body. Drink lots of water the day before and prior to your interview and ensure you have taken a bathroom break to avoid needing one while on the phone. If you have not spoken for several hours, do some voice exercises before your interview to have a clear and understandable tone. Clearing your throat when speaking on the phone can be a distraction and an annoyance to the person on the other end.

Smiling as you speak will make a huge difference in the delivery of your conversation. While it may seem that this is a silly practice, the difference between smiling and having a strait face can be heard. If you do not believe that this subtlety can be detected, do yourself a favor and record yourself speaking the same sentence twice. In one speak the words while smiling and in the second say the words as you would normally. Play both options back and hear the difference in the way the words are spoken.

Smiling as you talk about work you have been involved in, impacts you have had in your previous positions, things which motivate you, and when answering questions will provide a happy and uplifting tonality to your conversation which will be more engaging to your interviewer and show them you are a positive person. Smiling helps in any situation but when you are unable to make a physical impression, this is a wonderful tool which can make all of the difference in securing a second face to face interview or being passed by for the opportunity of a lifetime.

Chapter 6: Causes of Low Memory

Retention and Retrieval

Several factors influence your ability to retain information and retrieve it on time. This chapter discusses common factors that result in low memory retention and retrieval.

Stress

Stress directly affects your ability to form, consolidate, and retrieve memories. If you feel stressed out, you are likely to struggle a lot when forming short-term memories and while consolidating those short-term memories into your long-term memory. This is primarily because of the high cortisol levels present in the body whenever you feel stressed out.

The minute you perceive something as a threat to your wellbeing and survival, your brain triggers the fight or flight response aka the 'stress response' that creates a series of physiological reactions meant to help your body combat the stressful situation by fleeing from it or fighting it.

One physiological process that occurs during a stressful period is an increase in the cortisol levels. Cortisol is a stress hormone, which means as its levels rise, you experience a spike in your stress levels too. During a stressful situation, this is a helpful and much needed physiological response as it helps you battle the stressful demand effectively. However, if you feel unnecessarily frustrated and tensed for no reason, cortisol will keep circulating in your bloodstream, at which point it will do you more harm than good, and aggravate your stress levels.

One of the negative effects of this increased cortisol circulation is the inability to focus properly and think clearly because cortisol narrows your vision so that you can analyze things fast and often hastily. Naturally, when you are not focusing on something properly and cannot think things through, you will struggle with activating the necessary neuronal pathway at the right time, which will delay the time it takes you to recall a piece of information.

Moreover, stress affects your ability to recall a piece of information correctly. A study discovered that all the people who experienced or saw an event at the same time have dissimilar recollections of that experience. Every person's account and the amount of certainty they had about that event varied. This goes to show that memories tend to change once formed.

Each time you retrieve some memory, you tend to color it with your present experience of that memory. For instance, when you take a book off your bookshelf and place it back, you leave your fingerprints on that particular book.

Research also proves that when we question someone repeatedly about something and give the person false or somewhat confusing information about it, the information directly colors and clouds the person's memory. It even influences what they actually recall and in some instances, it may partially or completely modify already formed memories. If you have seen movies with courtroom drama or an interrogation scene, you know how a clever lawyer or detective when questioning a suspect tries to stress out the suspect as a strategy to influence his/her ability to recall the memory clearly.

Another study showed that stress directly hinders the memory formation process especially if a stress trigger occurs before or during the encoding process. This means if you underwent stress just as you are about to pick up information and encode it, it is likely you will be unable to recall that information because of the delay between encoding the information and consolidating it.

Moreover, stress causes mental and physical fatigue that in turn increases the likelihood of cognitive impairment that encompasses problems such as poor working memory and problems with staying attentive to a singular task.

If you often have problems with memorizing, retaining, and recalling information on time, it is likely you are under extensive stress or do not address your routine stress regularly which leads to chronic stress. If it goes unchecked for a long time, regular turns into chronic stress, anxiety, or even depression and continues to impede your ability to think clearly, form memories and then retain them. Stress obstructs your level of focus and when you cannot focus on something properly, you struggle with committing it to long-term memory and then recalling it when required.

To ensure you build killer focus and the ability to memorize and retrieve information effectively, work on managing your routine and chronic stress. The second part of this guide shall illustrate various strategies you can use to manage stress successfully and in so doing improve your brain.

Emotions and state of mind

Among the many factors that affect your ability to encode, consolidate and retain information, your emotional state holds great importance. Your emotions directly determine your ability to recall a memory quickly when you need to revisit it.

Various research studies have observed that an emotionally charged state of mind helps you easily encode a memory and retain it successfully when required. When you experience joy, anger, fear, or another intense emotion, you become emotionally involved in the experience at hand and create a long lasting memory of it.

Cognitive psychologist Donald McKay and his team of researchers worked on the impact of emotions on one's memory. They presented a group of participants with lots of dissimilar words to memorize. The research team printed every word in a dissimilar color and asked the participants to memorize and name the color. Later, they asked participants to remember the words on the card as well. McKay et al. discovered that 'taboo' words that elicited a strong emotional response in the subjects were quicker to recall in most participants compared to words that had a less intense emotional connotation.

This experiment and the many others conducted on emotional states and memory have clearly suggested that if you are in a strong emotional state when memorizing something, it positively influences your ability to encode that piece of information and commit it to your long-term memory. Moreover, if you coerce yourself into experiencing the same emotions when you wish to recall that information, you will retrieve it quite easily.

In 1977, researchers at the Harvard University published a paper titled 'Flashbulb Memories' that showed that people had vivid recollections of all events that held personal importance such as the assassination of John F. Kennedy, the death of Michael Jackson, and the terrorist attacks of 11*th* September, 2011. The study showed that every time you think of an event that holds personal significance, a moment of flashbulb memory occurs and you are able to retrieve that particular memory from your collection of memories quickly.

This means if you are not emotionally involved and immersed in an experience, and if you are unable to experience intense emotions at that time, you will not successfully encode, consolidate, and then retrieve that piece of information.

The evolutionary purpose of our emotion was to help us survive. In the past, intense emotions such as anxiety, fear, and rage helped our ancestors perceive danger at the right time and combat it successfully. A study showed that our emotions function beyond our conscious control, which heightens our intuition. This in turn helps us perceive potential threats on time or often beforehand and deal with them appropriately on time.

Research also shows that your brain focuses better on emotional stimuli. A study showed that when shown pictures displaying subjects with injuries, participants elicited a better emotional response that also resulted in a spike in their cognitive functioning compared to seeing ordinary images that did not elicit a strong emotional response.

This shows that if you want to enhance your ability to consolidate and retrieve information, you must become emotionally involved in the experience and build a strong, emotional connection with the piece of information.

Trauma

Various research studies have repeatedly proven that a traumatic episode greatly affects your ability to memorize and retain information. This is because during a traumatic event such as sexual assault, life-altering accident, or the loss of a loved one, your emotional state is highly activate and heightened. This consequently improves your focus on the event and all the central details pertinent to it stay vivid in your recollection of the experience. That said, lesser important information known as the 'peripheral details' may not be effectively retained. So you may recall the tool your assaulter used to hit you, but may not recall the other things he/she broke when trying to catch you.

When you experience a traumatic episode, your senses become highly stimulated, which means the brain effectively encodes into memory every piece of information you pick up with your five senses. Since trauma heightens your stress levels—you need cortisol to survive in that time—your ability to focus also improves which in turn helps you commit the information to long-term memory. If you recall that memory repeatedly, its neuronal pathways become stronger, which allows you to retrieve the information instantly whenever the need arises.

However, you must note that only the important pieces of information related to the traumatic event may be successfully encoded and other peripheral details like the location, date, exact time and details of the background may not be encoded and consolidated to your long-term memory.

Lack of Focus

If you are not fully attentive to a task or anything else you are trying to memorize and retrieve, you will struggle with the task. Your level of focus directly affects your ability to memorize and retain information. If you are multitasking when memorizing something or are constantly lost in thought and are just mechanically working on the task, it is likely you will not remember a word of what you are trying to memorize.

A good example of this occurs when kids try to learn something while watching cartoons at the same time. Because of being distracted and unfocused, they struggle for hours with memorizing a few words, but would hardly take minutes to memorize and then recall the same information when they focus solely on it.

Likewise, if your attention keeps switching from one thing to another, you experience 'attention-al blink,' which refers to a pause in your ability to focus attentively on something.

If this repeatedly occurs when you work on a task, it obstructs your level of focus, which then hampers your ability to memorize and consolidate information, and then effectively retain it when required. To improve your brainpower and memory, it is crucial to build laser focus.

Following chapters of the book will illustrate effective strategies you can use to become laser focused.

In addition to the above factors, various other elements influence the memory retention process; they include:

Too much/too little sleep

The amount and quality of sleep you get daily directly influences your memory. If you are not getting any sleep, you will have trouble retaining information and building long-term memories because the brain uses deep sleep cycles to keep important information into long-term memory.

A study from Harvard shows that over a period of six years, women who slept 5 or fewer hours and those who slept for 9 or more hours daily had poor to average scores on their brain tests compared to women who slept between 6 to 8 hours, which according to experts, is the average sleep requirement for adults.

Sleep deprivation affects the areas of your brain involved with emotional response, focus, and memory. If you do not get enough sleep daily, it will affect your cognitive development. Moreover, when you are sleep deprived, you feel fatigued and grumpy, which directly affects your ability to focus on tasks and think clearly, which consequently hampers your ability to learn things, encode information, and consolidate it.

Unhealthy Diet

Studies have proven repeatedly that a diet rich in processed foods and sugar leads to inflammation in the brain; this inflammation then paves way for short-term memory loss.

Foods such as, frozen pizza, coffee creamer, and frostings are rich in trans-fat that in turns damage the health of your brain. If you consume a diet rich in processed and other unhealthy types of food, this could be why you struggle with memorizing and retaining information.

Lack of Physical Activity

Experts also suggest that a lack of physical activity can cause poor memory retention. Working out and physical activity keeps the blood pumping to your brain tissue, which improves the production of growth hormones in your blood that in turn increases your brainpower.

If you live a purely sedentary lifestyle, this may be the reason why you have a tough time retaining information. You can improve on that by making room for regular exercise in your life.

Smoking

A study conducted by the McGill University discovered that regular smoking results in the thinning of the cortex, which as you already know is the part of your brain involved in forming and retaining memories. When your cortex thins out, your ability to form and retain memories deteriorates, which in turn affects your brainpower. If you are a regular smoker, seriously consider breaking this bad habit so that you can maintain a healthy brain as you age.

Now that you are well aware of all the various causes of poor memory and brain health, let us move to the second part of the book where we discuss ways to strengthen your brainpower.

Chapter 7: Avoiding the Negative

So far, we've covered what self-discipline is and where it comes from, and how time management is one of – if not *the only* – the key components of the personality trait. In this chapter, we'll be diverging a bit by talking not about the things you *should* do to become a more self-disciplined person, but rather some things you *shouldn't* do.

Self-discipline isn't just about cultivating good habits such as time management; it's also about doing away with the bad ones. Now, this book will be speaking in general terms because, again, everyone's personal goals and bad habits will differ. But regardless of all the many individual things that can chip away at a person's self-discipline, there are a few BIG things that many believe to comprise the main sources of a downfall for people who are trying to become more self-disciplined.

The first and foremost of these things is the dreaded excess. Depeche Mode once said, "Everything counts in large amounts." Well, allow me to just say that maybe Martin Gore had a little bit of a problem with excess and, as a result, could have used some self-discipline.

I don't mean to pick on Depeche Mode, because the truth is that excess really is something that many people find difficult to give up, especially in America which many people so optimistically see as being "the land of plenty." When it comes to the things they enjoy eating, or watching, or doing, a lot of people don't just lack self-discipline; they lack total self-control!

I know that before I began practicing self-discipline, my greatest foe was that pint of Ben & Jerry's ice cream that I could devour in just one sitting. You've probably had a similar experience, where that first taste of something or your first experience with a thing is just so good that, of course, you're going to have another. But again, this is a slippery slope and before you know it, you're running on autopilot. Part of me thinks that when we do this to ourselves, we're not even really enjoying the thing we're overindulging in; we just think we are because that first bite was so good, and we want to recapture that first taste again. But instead of putting down the ice cream, or turning off the video game – or, from chapter 2's example, getting off social media – we keep indulging. It's a shame, too, because if one would only cease the activity they've already had too much of, they could come back on it on another day and actually have a better chance of having that first, magnificent feeling again. Time apart does make the heart grow fonder, you know.

This is, of course, another problem that arises when we're passive about self-discipline rather than active. It's easy to do anything in excess when we're not paying attention or fully engaged with the given activity (eating, drinking, watching TV) despite that little nagging voice in the back of our heads that tell us we should probably stop.

Aside from making a schedule and sticking to it, I believe that avoiding excess really is the most difficult part of building up strong self-discipline. But, like time management, once you build up some good habits (in this case, the good habits are getting rid of the bad ones) things will start to get easier.

On the next page are some strategies you can employ that will help you to say "no" to overindulging.

1. Set a limit

The simplest solution is usually the most obvious, and that is definitely the case here. To keep yourself from having too much of something like an entire pint of Ben & Jerry's, you need to consciously tell yourself how much you're going to have, or rather, how much you will allow yourself to have. Think of this as a promise to yourself, and if you fail by going beyond the limit you've set, you will literally be lying to yourself, and no one wants that.

It doesn't matter what it is, be it TV, food, drinks; all you have to do is have a limit and once that limit is reached, you're done. Cut off. It doesn't matter if you're still hungry, or if that episode ended on the craziest cliff-hanger of all time. To have good, refined self-discipline, you need to have the ability to control what *you* are doing with yourself, and that means having the strength to tell yourself you've had enough.

If you need further help with this, you can even add certain things to your schedule from Chapter 2. For instance, if you tend to play video games or watch TV for way too long, you can set aside a block of time to do those things to make sure you don't overindulge.

2. Avoid temptation

For some, it isn't enough to just set a limit. Anyone who has ever been a recovering addict knows that to avoid relapsing into whatever it was they were addicted to, they need to refrain from ever going near that particular thing again if they wish to maintain their sobriety. Obviously, having a sweet tooth or watching too much TV isn't on the same level as being addicted to a potentially dangerous substance, but for people who just can't help themselves, the general principles can be applied.

For those who just can't help themselves, you need to understand that it's not a sign of weakness to avoid having things you tend to overindulge within your reach. In fact, taking the needed steps to remove those things from your life is a sign of strong self-discipline! Knowing that you lack self-control in a certain area and taking the necessary steps to compensate for that will help you build some very good habits in the long run.

As an example, I had a friend in high school who got into the video game, *World of Warcraft,* when it was at the peak of its popularity, and, although I'm no expert on addiction, I can say with a fair amount of confidence that he was, in fact, addicted to it. After getting home from school, he would rush to get his homework done before getting online. He would stay up late into the night playing the game, get a few hours of sleep in, then wake up before sunrise to get a few hours in before heading off to school. It eventually got to the point where we rarely saw one another outside of class. Luckily for him, when it got so bad that he was beginning to neglect his academic responsibilities, his parents took away his computer. After a month of going cold turkey, he told me he couldn't believe the amount of time he was pouring into that game, and when he eventually got his computer back, he uninstalled it.

Unlike my friend, most grown adults don't have their parents around to forcefully quell their overindulgence. Instead, it is up to them to realize when they're having too much of something, and it is up to them to do something about it even if that means cutting out the thing entirely.

3. Don't deny yourself life's little pleasures

As with most things in life, nothing is black or white. Usually, things fall into a grey area, and this certainly holds true for good and bad habits. I definitely don't want to give you the impression that having good self-discipline means giving up all the things you enjoy, such as sweet food, or a really good TV show. I love those things just as much as the next person, and our enjoyment of them makes life all the better.

What I am saying is that practicing moderation and avoiding excess are keys to making you a happier person because it allows you to enjoy a little bit of a lot of things in life as opposed a lot of just a few things. By doing this, you're more likely to find a higher feeling of satisfaction in experiencing these individual things while, at the same, time avoiding too much of any one of them.

In the end, though, it's all about balance. Having self-discipline doesn't mean you stop treating yourself; it means you've stopped going through the motions and that you're more aware of what kind of life you want for yourself. Therefore, if you schedule out a few times a week to exercise, you can absolutely have some ice cream at the end of a long day. If you work on that hobby of yours – a blog, a book, a painting, or whatever it is – you're allowed to veg out on the couch and watch an episode of that TV show you're hooked on. There isn't, however, any one way of deciding how much you should have because every person is different. It is up to you to decide what is a healthy amount of anything, and it's up to you to keep reevaluating yourself and your habits.

Now that you have a solid understanding of how you should avoid doing anything in excess, we will begin to look at how this manner of thinking, in conjunction with solid time management, will help you to start solidifying your good habits of self-discipline so you can ultimately start to reach your goals.

Chapter 8: The Art of Summarizing

Summarizing shouldn't be confused with the act of paraphrasing, which merely requires changing 1 or 2 sentences in order to express the same idea or message. Summarizing involves a process of shortening or abbreviating a resource material into a few number of words or sentences. Examples of summarizing include expressing the main ideas of a 10-page learning material into just 1 or 2 paragraphs, or expressing a paragraph or section's main points and ideas in just a sentence or two. Doing this gives you much freedom in terms of how to best concentrate on your learning materials according to a specific goal or need. It strips away the unnecessary substance and provides more focus on the more crucial information.

Summarizing is a great way to learn anything because it compels you to, among other things:

Spend meaningful time with your chosen learning material for condensing;

Think and study deeply about the learning material you chose to condense. It also compels you to distinguish between the significant points and ideas and those that aren't.

Express the learning material's main ideas and points in your own words, which in turn permits you to process the information well and learn them better from your own unique perspective.

Practice how to analyze better and think critically.

Process the important points and ideas of your learning materials

Mastering the Art of Summarizing

There are 3 steps involved here: retaining key ideas or points, discarding unimportant ones, and abbreviating your learning material by cutting away the not-so-important things like examples, details, descriptions, and narratives.

The amount of abbreviation or condensation needed for summarizing learning materials vary according to the purpose for summarizing (e.g., mental exercise, reference material in the future, information abstract, or study guide) as well as the amount of information available on the learning material. Some summaries condense original learning materials to about 30% of the original length or content to as compact as 5% only!

A good general guideline for summarizing learning materials is this: the greater the informational content of the material, the more condensed it should be. The logic behind it is that keeping the same condensation rate between a short reading material and a voluminous one will result in a very long and detailed summary for a voluminous learning material, which won't look anywhere near a summary anymore!

Take for example, 2 learning materials – a 5-pager and a 100-pager. Granting a similar condensation or summary rate of 20%, this means you'll only have to write a 1-page summary for the 5-page learning material. But for the 100-pager, that means you'll have to write a 20-page summary, which hardly qualifies as a summary anymore! Remember, the secret to making summarizing a great strategy for learning anything is this: keep it as brief as possible and consider only those ideas that are truly important. Simplicity is the main objective here.

Asking good questions also play a great role in being able to summarize well. These questions include, among others:

☐ Why do I need to summarize this material?

☐ What are the main ideas and points of this learning material?

☐ What is the single most important idea or point of this learning material?

☐ Which of these ideas or points can I afford to not include in the summary?

Chapter 9: History of Accelerated

Learning Techniques

Accelerated Learning Techniques

Accelerate learning is a method of learning that involves an individual being offered a program to learn at a faster pace than mainstream programs. The aim of accelerated learning is to offer individuals who excel in a specific subject the opportunity to learn at a quicker rate and also to learn more. Typically, there has always been a mainstream of ways to learn. Only recently has society started to adapt to the times and offered individuals who excel the opportunity to pursue their talents in a way that hasn't really been offered before.

Without a doubt, accelerate learning is a push in the right direction, because it encourages individuals and students to push themselves and not just settle for the mainstream, but to push for more by taking these accelerate classes and learning at an accelerated pace.

Suggestopedia

Dr. Georgi Lozanov was a Bulgarian professor who developed Suggestopdeia. This large word was generally used for individuals who were wanting to learn foreign languages quickly and effectively. Suggestopedia was a type of learning that involved creating a great and comfortable learning environment for an individual. Lozanov stressed that the key to an optimal learning environment was a teacher who truly cared about what they were teaching.

Suggestopedia was created in 1970, and was the concept that set the groundwork for accelerated learning. Accelerated learning still shares the same philosophies that Suggestopedia once did. The key concept being that Accelerated learning and Suggestopedia both remove the perceived limits that were set on an individual when it came to learning.

History of Learning

Throughout the entirety of the Human civilization, learning has always been paramount to our success and growth as a race. Although we have learned for thousands of years, it seems as if the rate at which we learn has always been at a constant pace, which is why we haven't really seen a technological boom or anything of the sorts until the last two centuries. The reason that we have seen more growth in the last two hundred years than the rest of our time on this Earth is because we have changed the way that we learn.

Accelerate learning has helped humanity loosen the learning chains set on us because it has given us the opportunity to separate ourselves from the mainstream in a way that has never happened before. Accelerated learning gives humanity a way to progress a quicker than ever before, and it is exciting what the future may hold for us.

Accelerated Learning for Business
Accelerated Learning

Throughout generations, learning has always been done in one way. It has been done in a slow pace that, although is thorough and makes sure an individual has the best opportunity to learn the specific piece of information that is being taught, it could be seen as relatively inefficient. Nowadays, accelerated learning has changed the way we learn. Accelerated learning has made it possible to learn at a quicker pace, which offers an individual, as well as a business the chance to excel even more so in a subject that they are already doing well in. Accelerated learning is without a doubt the future. Look at how much the human civilization has developed within the last two centuries compared to the rest of the time humans have been on this planet. It is insane how much we've developed.

How can Accelerated Learning help my Business?

Accelerated learning is not just for individuals, it is also performed by businesses. Accelerated learning can help a business through teaching the people who work for the business, how to do their job in a much more efficient manner. It should be noted that accelerated learning is a much more vigorous type of learning compared to any other, but this is why it is so effective. It can help a business by pushing workers to their limits through accelerated learning.

Can it help my Business, not just the Workers?

Of course, accelerated learning is not just for the development of individuals, businesses can thrive off of the technique of accelerated learning. Imagine a business that is new and up and coming. The only problem is that they are unsure of how to get started and what they need to know. With accelerated learning, a business has the opportunity to learn how to be successful and make money in an efficient and timely manner that won't stall the company's progress in any significant manner.

In the past, people had to learn things for years before they could ever think about opening up their own business or anything like that. Of course, it's still a good idea to study about what you want to do first, however, with accelerated learning it won't take years upon years to just simply learn how to start up your own business. It is extremely hard work compared to any other program available, but at the end of the day, if you are willing to put in the work then you are bound to reap the rewards.

Chapter 10: Strengthening Photographic Memory

T
raining your memory skills is not difficult. In fact, even a child can learn some of the following techniques without too much hassle or effort.

These tips will not only help you improve your memory but will also help you be able to recall information at a much quicker rate.

Minimize distractions – Being able to minimize things that distract you is perhaps one of the best ways to truly develop a superb skill in recalling memory. Do not blame your forgetfulness on memory, but rather turn the blame to the long lists of distractions that plague us each and every day. Do your best to focus and hone in on one thing at a time, instead of trying to take in multiple things all at once.

Improve your lifestyle – Many memory issues that we face are due to our body's response to anger, depression, anxiety and other such feelings. It is important, not only for your recall rate but also for your overall well-being to keep the symptoms of these ailments at bay, for they harm you in much more ways than one. Ensure that you spend plenty of time doing things that you love and learn from.

Go out and get more physical exercise – Physical activity helps increase the flow of blood to every part of our body, and this does not exclude the brain. Exercise allows more of those essential nutrients along with more oxygen to reach our brains so that they too can perform better! 30 minutes of exercise 5 days a week is plenty. But more is better.

Keep your mind active – Just like all the other muscles in our body, if we do not use it, we lose it. The same goes for our complex brains. The more we use it, the better it will perform when we really need it to. Try to incorporate some of these brain-stimulating activities throughout your week, to get your brain off of autopilot and on to something more invigorating.

Learn how to play an instrument

Learn a new language

Play a board game

Read the newspaper or a book

Perform crossword puzzles

Visualization – The terms of utilizing visualization can improve your memory retention ten-fold. Ensure that you practice visualization techniques and use image associations on a regular basis.

Military techniques – There are some vital tricks that our own military utilizes when in combat, including psychic spying and objective viewing. They can remember coordinates, locations, and images with these techniques, which are vital not only for their survival but there mission and other combat mates.

Courses and exercises – Thanks to the broad span of the World Wide Web, there are hundreds of courses and things you can do to improve your memory. This could be from picture games, telling stories, building lists, and word association exercises. These games make it seem like you are not even learning or practicing memory retention and are pretty darn effective at getting the job done.

Become self-directed – You and only you can be the one to take control of what you get out of the knowledge you acquire and what you get from it. Ask questions if needed! There are plenty of ways to obtain resources to receive the help you need! The more you inquire, the faster you learn things.

Build up your background knowledge – When we take the time and initiative to learn things on our own accord, the more quality of learning one actually gets in the long run.

Create a good learning discipline – When you go into your sessions of memory training, you need to go in with a mind clear of all other distractions. Easier said than done, I know. Multi-tasking, no matter how beneficial our society claims it is, is not to be done while undergoing memory sessions. This also means while you are putting your learning curves into practice in real life as well. If your mind is preoccupied, this leaves very little room to actually conduct a photographic memory session in its completion. Do not divide up your attention into various sections. Keep your attentive eye on that memorizing prize!

Determine your learning objectives – Whenever you finally get the spark to acquire any new knowledge, it is important to ask yourself why you want to learn this and if it is worth your time and energy. Determine your purpose of learning and practicing something. This way, you will pay better attention and give it more special recognition as you go along.

Memory strategies

Utilize image associations – This tip especially comes in handy for attempting to locate something that you cannot find. If you are looking for a book or car keys, take a second to imagine where they would be. If you book is perhaps called "A Hundred Suns," visualize what a hundred of those suns would appear like. Imprinting images within your mind can help you recall the book and perhaps find it later.

Repetition of names – If you are one that struggles with recalling people's names or names of certain things, you are not the only one. Many people have a hard time retaining names, especially when trying to remember more than one or two names at once.

After meeting someone, repeat their name back to them. "It is so nice to meet you 'so-so.'" If you did not hear their name correctly or didn't hear quite how they pronounced it, clarify it right then to avoid asking it again later, saving yourself the embarrassment.

Learn to associate newly acquired names with someone you already know with the same name. If you do not know someone personally by that name, think of characters in books or favorite films. This association assists with recalling the names later.

Utilize 'chunking' – Even though this technique sounds more like an issue that your car is having, it is a psychological phrase about a memory retention process that involves the clumping together of items, words, numbers, etc. on the same list to ensure you remember them.

If attempting to memorize your grocery list, put all items into categories, such as fruits, veggies, frozen, condiments, meats, etc. Or, you can even categorize lists by meals you are going to make from the items you are trying to memorize.

Dividing sets of specific numbers into smaller sections will help you recall telephone, social security, credit card numbers, etc. Instead of trying to remember an entire sequence of numbers, divide them up into sections. For example, instead of 1234567890, memorize it as 123-456-7890. This will assist you in repeating it back to yourself to ensure proper memorization of it.

Get out those UNO cards – Or any deck of cards, for that matter. Whichever deck suites you're fancy! You will be utilizing them for a while, so choose wisely. Draw the top three cards and try to memorize those cards. Then place those three back into the deck at random and spread them out. From the spread-out deck, choose your three cards and put them in the same order that they were earlier. Perform this exercise with three cards for a week, five the next, then continue to increase your card count each week. Do this until you can memorize the entire deck in one sitting.

Domino trick – With a box of dominos make a pattern out of 10 of them. Memorize that pattern. Each week thereafter add 10 more dominos to your pattern. Do so until you can use the entire box. This method takes a while!

Picture engraining – This method is one used by our military to learn names and recognize faces quickly. You must not miss a day, or you have to perform this exercise for another week. You will need:

A piece of paper that contains a cut-out box the size of 1 paragraph

A paragraph of words you choose

Windowless room

Small but bright light

Head to your darkened room and set up your light, turn it on and proceed to set up your paragraph so that the hole of your box covers up everything but the paragraph you wish to memorize. Look at the paragraph in front of you for 5 minutes. Turn off the light while you are still staring at the page. Repeat this same process each and every day for a month or until you can recall the paragraph in its entirety without any mistakes. This process utilizes light to engrain the visual of what you want to memorize into your brain.

Honing your Eidetic Memory Capabilities

Since we have discussed many ways to develop your photographic memory skills, we might as well touch base about a technique you can use to better your eidetic memory skills as well!

Training your brain to memorize in eidetic ways is not complicated, but it must be exercised in three ways: **speed, space, and quantity**.

Speed – This technique was created to train the speed at which you perceive and remember what you have seen. The idea is to make the amount of time you need to memorize shorter and shorter.

Utilize a program on your computer that lets you view something for short periods of time. Show things for 1o seconds to start out. And decrease over time as you grasp the training.

Space – The goal of this technique is to exercise the brain to memorize things that are separated by just a space that is big yet small enough for your eyes to visualize and memorize in a single glace. The idea of the space exercise is to memorize things without eye movement.

Write down a phone number that you can read in a single eyeshot. Ensure that you are only using your peripheral vision. To really train yourself to utilize this technique, using a computer program that shows stuff in a separated way, both height and width, is best. Start with shorter distances, gradually working your way up to farther distances while taking in more information.

Quantity – The goal of this technique is to memorize and remember as much information as you possibly can.

Utilize a computer program that provides you with items to memorize and gradually increase the number of subjects while lessening the time you must do so. If you do not wish to use a program, writing or typing out telephone numbers is another great way, adding more numbers as you decrease your memorization time.

Chapter 11: Anatomy of the Brain- How the Hippocampus Works for Long- and Short-term Memory

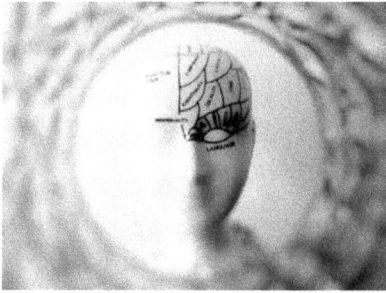

Can you recall the name of every elementary school teacher you had? Or are you the sort that gets all the way to work before realizing you left your lunch at home? Memory is a funny thing, and we tend to categorize ourselves as either having a good memory or a bad memory. That's an oversimplified view of a cerebral function that has many forms and many purposes.

Some people are exceptional at remembering names and faces, and some people have thousands of song lyrics imprinted in their minds. Some people would, as they say, forget their head if it wasn't attached, and some people are the proverbial steel trap. Which are you, and which do you strive to be? Before you begin making your 'memory goals', let's take a look at how the brain is constructed, how memories are formed and where the brain stores them for recall.

Overview of the Brain

The human brain is made up of four main segments; the cerebrum, the cerebellum, the medulla, and the pons. Each segment has smaller areas which have very specific tasks, and all the parts work together to make the brain function properly.

The cerebrum is the largest, uppermost part of the brain, and is split into left and right hemispheres. Each hemisphere has four lobes: the parietal lobe, which governs spatial orientation; the frontal lobe, which is responsible for decision-making and judgement; the temporal lobe, which processes hearing, language, and memory; and the occipital lobe, which takes care of visual processing.

The cerebellum is underneath the cerebrum and sits on top of the brain stem at the origin of the spinal column. The cerebellum's main function is to regulate equilibrium and muscle coordination.

The pons is a messenger. It handles communication between the cerebellum, the cerebrum, and transmits information down the spinal cord. Lastly, the medulla controls involuntary actions like heartbeat and breathing.

Each of the four main components of the brain are intertwined with smaller components that all have a specific function. The pituitary gland governs endocrine function, while the amygdala processes involuntary emotions. We're going to focus on the hippocampus, which is located deep inside the temporal lobe of the cerebrum. The hippocampus plays a vital role in the storage of long-term memories. By discovering how this vital brain component functions, you'll be able to see why it's so crucial in the learning process. In the graphic below, you'll see the mains parts of the brain marked out according to their functions. Each section is highly specialized to perform certain tasks which make up the whole of the human brain's activity.

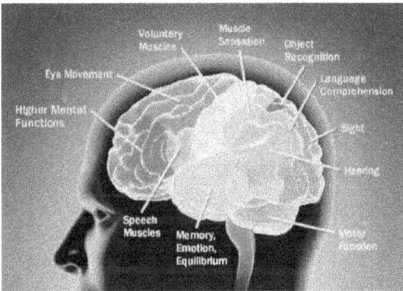

The Brain, Sorted by Function
The Hippocampus
The hippocampus, as we've just learned, is the part of the brain which governs long-term memory. It is divided into two halves, with each half sitting on one side of the line between the hemispheres of the brain. This small portion of the organ is responsible for forming and storing long-

term memories, mentally cataloging new surroundings, and filing away statistical facts, likes names and numbers.

Damage to the hippocampus can cause memory loss, and patients with Alzheimer's disease show significant loss of function in the hippocampus. As part of the body's limbic system, the hippocampus also aids with spatial awareness and emotional responses.

When the hippocampus is functioning properly, it's the area of the brain where long-term memories are stored. Short-term memories are not a function of the hippocampus; the cerebral cortex and cerebellum handle those memories, as well as handling procedural memories, such as walking or running. The hippocampus also does not seem to be involved in the process of learning a new skill.

There are two types of memory loss which can occur with traumatic damage to the hippocampus. Retrograde amnesia means the temporary or permanent loss of long-term memories. Anterograde amnesia is the inability to form or store any new memories.

The Hippocampus Uses Filing Cabinets

The hippocampus itself is made up of three segments, which are almost like file cabinets. The dorsal hippocampus stores spatial information, as well as verbal and conceptual memories. The ventral hippocampus files away conditioned behaviors and fear responses. The intermediate hippocampus functions as a go-between and manages overflow from the dorsal and ventral sections. That is to say, the intermediate hippocampus displays characteristics of the other two parts, and seems to exist to be able to function in either manner.

How Does the Filing System Work?

The functions of the brain have been studied for decades and while neuroscientists are still trying to figure out everything the brain does and everything it can do, researchers have known for many years that the hippocampus is a long-term storage facility.

The hippocampus stores experiential memories by taking data from the brain's processing centers, like the frontal cortex, and encoding that data as 'autobiographical'. The hippocampus is where your brain stores things like your early childhood memories, your first crush, or mental images of your first car. The hippocampus relies heavily on the sensory information it receives to determine if a long-term memory is, in essence, worth creating.

In relation to those long-term memories, there's strong evidence to suggest that the hippocampus takes emotional information from the amygdala and stores it as emotional memories. This is one of the reasons that strong memories have the ability to evoke the same emotional reaction as the day the memory was imprinted. These emotional memories could be triggered by something like hearing your wedding song, or visiting an important place from your childhood.

The hippocampus also specifically stores spatial memories that it encodes from the processing centers of the brain, such as the medial cortex. These spatial memories can be of the layout of a specific location, or navigational memories. Cab drivers have been shown to have increased activity in the areas of the hippocampus that store spatial memories, possibly due to the constant reinforcement of regular routes and the subsequent memorization of those routes.

It's the loss of the spatial memories in the hippocampus which is often associated with dementia and Alzheimer's. The damage to the hippocampus linked with those diseases can lead to disorientation and confusion. Injury or traumatic damage can also cause the loss of spatial memories.

What Else Can Affect the Hippocampus?

Injury and dementia-type diseases are not the only issues that can negatively affect the hippocampus's ability to create and store long-term memories. Studies show that post-traumatic stress disorder (PTSD) and mental illnesses such as schizophrenia and severe clinical depression can cause an atrophy of the hippocampus. Such an atrophy can cause a loss of recall of long-term memory, an inability to form and store new memories, memory distortion, and cognitive problems.

Stress and the so-called 'stress hormone' cortisol can also affect how the hippocampus stores and forms memories. High cortisol levels are also associated with endocrine disorders such as Cushing's syndrome. In many of these cases, lost hippocampal function can be partially or fully restored through pharmaceutical treatment of the underlying condition(s).

Epilepsy can also cause damage to the hippocampus and prompt loss of memory. The brain cells which misfire and cause epileptic seizures often suffer from hyperexcitability which can lead to cell death. Ischemic strokes can have a similar effect. Both epilepsy and strokes, as well as loss of blood flow to the brain have been linked to transient global amnesia, a sudden total loss of memory. Diagnostic imaging of patients with TGA often show small lesions on the hippocampus after the event. TGA often reverses course as suddenly as it occurs, with little or no permanent damage to the hippocampus.

The Inner Workings of Short-term Memory
When an event, a fact, or a mental image isn't deemed worthy of going into long-term storage, that doesn't mean it isn't a necessary piece of information. We use our short-term memory every day- to remember a phone member as we dial it, to order lunch for our coworkers, or to recall a dollar amount to write out a check at the mechanic.

Short-term memory has a very small retention window, about 20-30 seconds total. It also only has the capacity to store about seven items, like the digits of a phone number or a short shopping list. The brain only keeps those items on deck while we need them, and then the memory flees. It's only when we consistently use those items that they become committed to long-term memory. Before the advent of cellular phones, which store all our contact information for us, this might be a number you dialed frequently or an address to which you often wrote.

Short-term memory is based in synaptic function. As the brain takes in and processes stimuli, it creates a synaptic response. As the neurons and axons fire, the data moves down the line of cells until it essentially fizzles out. The brief duration can be reset by reading or reciting the information again. Memory 'chunking' can also help restart the clock on a short-term memory. This entails breaking down the needed information into smaller pieces of data.

The most common example of chunking is a standard ten-digit phone number. Observe this string of numbers:

9735551234

And this one:

973-555-1234

By breaking the digits into groups, the brain can more easily interpret and recall the data as a whole. Other examples of this might be trying to memorize a social security number or account information.

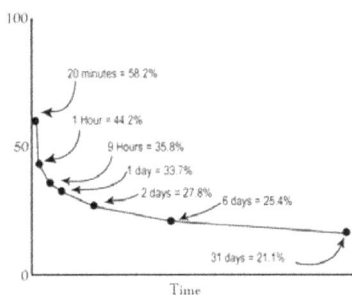

The graph shown below is known as an Ebbinghaus Memory Curve, or 'forgetting curve'. It shows the speed at which a short-term memory is lost, and how the recall of information levels off over time. The chart, which was developed by German psychologist Hermann Ebbinghaus in the mid-1880s, does not account for any additional rehearsal of information- simply a piece of data given once and then tested for recall over the specified time period. Rehearsal or practice is typically accounted for and depicted by a learning curve, also developed by Ebbinghaus. He also conducted pioneering research on learning, leaning heavily on the theory of spaced repetition and using mnemonic devices.

Ebbinghaus Memory Curve

What About Working Memory?

Somewhere between the fleeting nature of short-term memory and the staying power of long-term memory is the middle ground of working memory. Working memory is a cocktail of sorts, part new information, part stored data, part cognitive function, and part rapid processing.

When we refer to working memory, an example might be completing a new task at work. You're familiar with your company's policies and procedures, and you know that based on that knowledge, you can complete the new work- that's your long-term memory. You are also processing information pertinent to the new task- perhaps a new software program that needs to be learned on the fly to meet a deadline, and you've committed the password to that program to your short-term memory.

Now, imagine your feelings on Day 1 of the new project. You're feeling a little nervous, you're trying to take in a lot of information at once, and you're trying to calm down and rely on your experience. Jump to Day 5. You've begun to get the hang of it, and you're handling the task with much more ease. You've acclimated to the software, and you've gotten to know the data a little better. All the things that were thrown at you on the first day have started to become familiar. You've built a working memory.

The question now becomes, will that working memory become a long-term memory? That's up to the cortex and the hippocampus. If the frontal cortex determines from the available data that the task you've been training in is a one-time deal, the process may not be committed to the hippocampus. If the work is something that is becoming part of your everyday job going forward, or is something you'll be asked to complete regularly, it will be filed away as a long-term memory.

Practice and repetition are the keys to the evolution of a memory from short-term to working to long-term. In the next chapter, we'll delve into the hows and whys of practice and studying, and how best to apply your efforts to make maximum strides in your learning goals.

Chapter 12: Computer Role in Accelerated

Learning

Accelerated Learning

Accelerated learning is the way forward. It is the best way to learn in this day and age, where everything happens at such at such a rapid pace. If everything else is so fat, why shouldn't the rate at which we learn to be quick as well? It only makes sense, really. Computers are the one of the key reasons why the world has sped up. The internet and electronic devices in general have enabled us as a race to communicate with people across the other sides of the world in seconds. Computers also have helped us learn quicker. Here are a few ways that computers have helped accelerate the rate at which we learn.

Everything you need to Know, in One Place

The great thing about a computer is that it holds literally everything you will ever need to learn within itself or on the internet. This is important, because before computers it was considered difficult to accumulate all the information that you needed to efficiently learn something. Learning used to be a slow process, but thanks to computers and accelerated learning, this is no longer the case. Forget having to look through dozens of books to simply find a few points that you are looking for. With computers, simply search what you are wondering and it is likely that you'll find the information and understand it within minutes.

Computer's Accelerate Learning

Perhaps a key example of how computers can speed up the way that we learn is through watching YouTube videos. The videos offer two of your senses the opportunity to learn something. You get to hear something and see it. Although you could already do this if you had a teacher, with videos and YouTube you can learn whatever you want efficiently and effectively without ever having to interact with anyone else. Accelerated learning and computers have helped people build an independence when it comes to their learning.

Computer's Role

A computer's role in accelerated learning is to literally accelerate it. If you want to learn slowly and like everyone else, you will follow the mainstream and go to class, learn from a teacher with people who aren't really passionate about what they are being taught. The quality of learning is low and slow. With computers, it gives you the opportunity to only rely on yourself. When you are only relying on yourself, you dictate the quality as well as the amount of time it takes to learn. Computers allow you to accelerate your learning as quickly as you want to

Chapter 13: How to read faster by

understanding what you read

Autumn is the time to return to routine, to classes if you are still a student, to read and not so much for pleasure, but for obligation.And there, sometimes we would like to be like the ' Short Circuit ' robot and read three books in five minutes, but our brains do not work that way. Although you can be trained to read faster and to understand what you read , that is the great *crux* of the matter. Because reading very fast and not knowing anything, in the end, it is as if we did not know how to read.

The average reading speed is considered to be between 200 and 300 words per minute , but for each person it may be different. Not only will it depend on how accustomed we are to read, whether we do it in our mother tongue or another, whether the vocabulary used is familiar or unknown, whether around us there are external factors that distract us ... It will also depend Of how trained our eyes are to read.

The eye is slower than the brain

"The ideal would be to be able to read as quickly as the thought arises, which is always much faster than the process of visual perception." Juan Guerrero, points out a method to improve reading comprehension that includes techniques for students, above all, to learn to read faster.The eyes are much slower reading than the brain is processing that information, so it ends up "distracting".

When we read, our eyes do not follow the text in a continuous way, but rather do it in jumps (called "eye jumps") and making pauses (called "eye breaks"). They also stop at fixation points where they read blocks of meaning, which can be a word, a group of words or an entire sentence. The more fixation points are made, the slower the reading , the more interruptions there will be in the flow of information to the brain and the understanding of the text will be worse.

The "trick", therefore, is to train the eyes to make more fluid movements when reading, so that they do not stop so much at the attachment points. Guerrero explains about that slow reading speed that:

"Usually the slow reader, who reads at a rate of about 150 to 200 words per minute, or speaks speech aloud or mentally during the course of his reading, has a bad habit of reading On the one hand, slows down the reading speed, with the consequent loss of time, and on the other hand, it ensures a poor understanding of the thought expressed in the text, since the slow reading, "word for word" , Breaks the thought into small pieces, which makes it impossible, or extremely difficult, to grasp globally in its fluid becoming.

A higher reading speed is associated with better reading comprehension , and in pursuit of that faster reading, the goal is to understand whole sentences , not get stuck in loose words. But before we start giving advice on how we can read more quickly, we will have to find out if we are slow or fast readers.

STOP Subvocalization

One of the mistakes most of us make when reading is that of subvocalization.

What is subvocalization? Simply mentally repeat each word as you read. The effect is that this way it is not possible to read at more than 150 words per minute. Which is a very low value if you want to save reading time or read much more.

To give you an idea, the average reader reads about 250 words per minute (or ppm op / m). This means that at times he is not mentally repeating the words he reads.

I say "in some moments" because eliminating the subvocalization, the reading speed is triggered and the 250 ppm can be very very short.

If you subvocalize, you are mentally repeating the words one by one as you read. The images (words) captured by your eyes, go through the acoustic system (the ear) and from there to the brain.

When you do not subvocalize, this is what happens: you eliminate a step, that of (mentally) hearing the words you read. The result, you read much faster.

And how to eliminate subvocalization?

This will require at least another book but for now tell you to try the following:

Count from 1 to 10 and repeat: "one, two, three, ..., nine, ten, one, two, ..."

Repeat one syllable constantly: "la, la, la, la, la ..."

Listen to instrumental music that does not sound like anything.

Read faster, just that

Actually all this is based on practice. With it, you will not need to do any of the first three points to not mentally repeat what you read. In the first attempts you get do not subvocalize (not mentally repeat what you read) you will see that your reading speed will have been high, but surely you have not stayed with much of what you read. Do not worry! Practice is the key.

What kind of reader are you?

Are you a bookworm like Rory Gilmore and you take two different books to read on the subway? To know if you can be Usain Bolt readers there are tricks that can guide you about your reading speed . What is usually done is to take a reference text, for example, from the superclass eclipse a few weeks ago:

A total superclass eclipse consists of two phenomena. On the one hand, there is a full moon in the perigee, that is, the closest point of the natural satellite to Earth. The Moon's orbit is not round at all, and when it reaches that close position, it looks 14% larger than normal. This is what is known as superluna.

On the other hand, we have a lunar eclipse or what is the same: when the Earth is placed between the Sun and the Moon so that our planet blocks the light that reaches the satellite. In solar eclipses it happens the other way round: it is the Moon who puts in between and creates those beautiful images where we see how it stands for a few moments before the star king.

During a lunar eclipse, the satellite crosses the shadow of the Earth. It consists of two zones: the umbra and the penumbra. In the penumbra you can see how the Moon enters and leaves the absolute darkness that is the umbra since in the latter the light does not reach. Therefore, when the satellite begins to hide in the lunar eclipse will give the feeling that it fades and little by little will disappear.

As the Moon approaches the umbra, from Earth we will see that when it reappears it will do so with a very intense ocher and red tone. This is known as the moon of blood, a rare phenomenon that in its day was related to superstitions and legends around the world. To this day science has already explained precisely why it occurs.

We count the words of that text, which in this case are 280, and we time what it takes to read them. Then we divide the number of words by the seconds that has led us to read them, and multiply the result by 60. Thus we will get the number of words per minute we read , that if they are between 100 and 200, they are a slow speed, between 200 and 300 , The average, and above 400, a fast speed.

HOW TO READ FASTER

Juan Guerrero points out that "the good reader, who does not vocalize and is able to grasp three or more words with a single glance, will be able to grasp the meaning of words by relying on the context , so that the fast reader can read very quickly Without compromising the perfect interpretation of words and understanding of the text, "and it is a capacity that can be learned and trained.

The first thing we usually do is try to eliminate the "vices" or bad habits that we may have developed while reading, and that slow us down. We must discover what is preventing us from reading quickly and efficiently. "Our bad reading habits (vocalization, subvocalization, excessive fixation, setbacks, etc.) should be discovered and eradicated," says Guerrero, who later explains that the visual method of Progrentis "is a specialized ocular and cerebral training program that can Five-fold speed and reading comprehension, "and consists of three levels: Mentor 1, which improves the decoding of the text by working the eye fixations; Mentor 2, which improves reading comprehension through reading operations, and Mentor 3, which improves retention through mnemonics.

With quick reading, the reader is expected to have an overall understanding of the text, and not be stuck in loose words

Of course, there are also *apps* and tools that help increase our reading speed, like Spritz. For example, it is recommended not to speak the words quietly while reading them and avoid re-reading passages that we have just read. We must also try to develop a broad spectrum of reading, ie read several grouped words, and even use a guide to force our eyes to follow, and prevent them from jumping back and pausing.

Felipe Bernal, creator of the method '21 reading errors that you should never commit to read fast with good understanding and how to solve them ', points out a technique to read faster based on a smaller number of fixations : "It is convenient to try to decrease the number Of fixations with which we read.A normal reader makes as many fixations as there are white spaces between the words (...) A quick reader mentally divides each line into the fixations that he finds comfortable.

The trick is, in part, not to read words. The Center of Professors and Resources of Mérida has a guide for the fast and efficient reading that affirms that:

"Reading words is a useless practice and a serious hindrance to true reading.Never should we ever read words, let alone go further in our reading word for word, in reality.In fact our vision is capable of capturing sets of words, two , Three and even more with an adequate training and of these, only its image, of global form ".

Some tricks for quick reading

It is common for us to find exercises and tricks of a different kind so that we can put into practice a greater speed of reading , which are then accompanied by some questions about the text we have read to determine if we have understood it or if we have simply seen words without Understand its meaning. We can, for example, include incomplete words in a sentence, to force us to look at a group of them in order to understand it:

During an ecl pse rn on the s te s, the T er a

Another option is to cover with a leaf the words, leaving only visible the top . It allows us to perform what is called " spatial reading, " because our brain is able to "fill in" missing information and identify those words, and concepts, seeing only the top half.

What is sought is that we capture the ideas of the text , rather than the words. We can force ourselves to read faster, although at first we do not fully understand the text, using a card with a hole in the center, that only let us see a line of that text. We are going down it with a certain rhythm, and a little higher of our habitual reading speed, to be obliged to reduce the fixations, to obtain a global image of the phrase instead of focusing on the individual words.

Fast reading and the modern world

We may wonder why it is necessary for us to learn to read faster without losing the ability to comprehend the text. Juan Guerrero himself explains that:

"We live in the Age of Knowledge Society, a society immersed in technology and digital content, where access to knowledge is universal and digital writing is immediate and borderless. All this is opening a gap in learning, speed Which I must learn is being exponentially separated from the speed at which I can learn. "

The Internet has widened that gap more and more, and if a professional wants to continue forming and keeping abreast with the innovations of his work, he has no choice but to search and read much information. Guerrero points out that "reading ability develops throughout primary education, reaching maturity at this stage (approximately 10-11 years) as the reading technique is usually no longer perfected. Vocabulary and the understanding of more complex topics, but not the amount of information that can be read . However, the amount of information that a person should read, for their personal and professional development, increases throughout life. This gap between what I can and should read motivates learning deficits. "

The PISA report, which assesses students' competence in various fields at an international level, included for the first time in 2009 the digital reading , or what is the same, reading on the internet (which includes browsing through its pages and handling Of hyperlinks) and electronic texts. In 2012, the report found that, in general, "student achievement in digital reading is closely related to reading performance," and concluded that "students' interest and skills in digital reading could be used to initiate A 'virtuous circle' through which a more frequent reading of digital texts would translate into better results in reading, which in turn would lead to a greater enjoyment of reading and also to better results in print reading. "

HOW TO better Remember What we read

We all have a favorite book, one that we have read many times and that always makes us have a good time, or leads us to think, or elicits interesting conversations with other people. However, we are not always able to remember exactly some of the things we have read in that book, or in a story in the newspaper that we liked. We read something that interests us, but then we tend to forget much of it.

There are ways we can better remember what we just read. We do not have to face a text as if we were going to study it for a test, but there are recommendations we can follow to improve our retentive capacity when we read. Most are rather simple and even common sense advice, as it were, and we do not need to believe in our head a palace of memory , as did Hannibal Lecter.

The pillars of memory

The keys to remembering information that we have just received are based on the three principles of memory: printing, association and repetition . Our brain better remembers that which "impresses" it, which generates in it some remarkable image or sensation. When we read, we can help to make that impression by reading some passages aloud , for example, using sound as a support for memory.

Luis García Carrasco, author of the book 'The Art of Memory' , and the podcast of the same title , points out among his tips for memorizing that 'we remember the things that have made some impression on us', and advocates that we use imagination to To make associations that allow us to remember certain things that until that moment were unknown to us.

The association refers to the connection of that new information that we are receiving with something that we already know of before. Familiarity with the topic we are reading is crucial for our brain to retain more or less data. "It is not the same to read about something that is unknown , rather than about

118

something that does. The brain retains more information about something that we do know, " says Enrique Castillejo, president of the Official College of Pedagogues and Psychopedagogues of the Community of Valencia .

Our brain remembers better what it is already familiar with, so if we read something totally new to us, it will cost us more to retain it

The third pillar on which memory is based is repetition . If we read the same passage several times, we will most likely remember it later. These three principles are also behind our retentive capacity in dealing with a new text, which we have to make more familiar and close to us. That is why it is often advised that we imagine ourselves doing some of the things that are said in that text, or associate them with something we already know, or emphasize passages and take notes .

Learn to read

In 1940, the American philosopher Mortimer Adler published How to Read a Book , a bestseller that explained how to make the most of the Great Books of Human History, a project in which he had participated with Robert Hutchins of The University of Chicago, which consisted of the elaboration of a canon of the most important works of Western literature. In his book, Adler gave several tips for a critical and analytical reading of books, and to remember much of what we read in them.

The philosopher explained that there were four different levels of reading: elementary, inspection, analytic, and syntactic . These levels are cumulative, going from the most general and superficial to the deepest

·Elementary level : Adler presented it with the question what does the book say? It is the first contact with him.

·Level of inspection : What is the book about? The reader has to extract all possible information from the surface of the book, looking for the chapters that seem fundamental, trying to classify it from its title and its preface, estimating the range of themes through its index, etc.

·Analytical level : What does the book mean? It is a more systematic reading and involves the underlining of some passages, the taking of notes in the margins, notes on the concepts handled in the book and its structure.

·Syntopic level : How does this book compare with others? That is, we are faced with comparative reading of the book. The reader uses his previous readings to analyze the work in question looking for a common terminology, defining the topics treated, looking for the most relevant passages. It is the most active level.

In analytic and syntactic reading is where the reader has to work more. At these levels , note-taking, underlining, or any other way of highlighting notions that allow us to focus our attention on them, and then writing a summary of what we have read, an attempt to analyze what I wanted Tell the author of the book.

Enrique Castillejo also recommends this to improve our retentive capacity:

"The important thing is not to worry about the speed of reading, but when we finish a unit of content (which can be a chapter), we can write a summary of what we just read."

The environmental factors

The most common advice, if we want to remember better what we read, is always "pay attention". Concentrating on the task we are doing obviously increases the chances that our brain gets an impression, associates it with something it already knows, and ends up remembering it with a couple of repetitions. However, there may be external, environmental constraints that favor this more in-depth reading, to help us focus.

There are many recommendations in that regard, since we change our stay from time to time so our brain does not settle (and that not all psychologists fully support because there is no evidence that it really works) to the advice of Luis García Carrasco, Which states that being relaxed is also very important before we get to read because it provides us "greater facility to memorize and understand what we read."

In his book, he proposes a trick to help us concentrate , consisting of sitting in a chair where we are comfortable, closing our eyes, breathing deeply and paying attention to our breathing. Although it seems that we start thinking about something else, nothing happens; We focus again on the breath and stay that way for about five minutes, which will help us relax and concentrate better.

The environment is important to help us acquire that relaxation and that concentration that will facilitate our capacity of retentive reading. "It takes a propitious environment," says Enrique Castillejo, who adds that "natural light fatigues less, reads better seated ..." We have to create the ideal conditions to get us to read , although there are also trained readers able to make a Reading more or less analytical in the middle of a huge noise, for example, or in places where there may be many distractions.

Tips to remember what we read

We could say that there are several recommendations that can help us to better remember what we are reading, or what we have just read. Above all, what will make it easier for us to pay attention to the book or text that we have in hand, and that we do not find it difficult to retain the main thing.

· Look for a quiet place, with good lighting and where you can read comfortably.

· Do not worry about being the quickest to read the book; Each person has a different reading speed to understand what he is reading.

· Highlight the passages of the text that interest you. It can be done by underlining or, in digital readers, changing the typography of those phrases to highlight more about the rest.

· Look for associations of what you are reading with events that have happened to you.

· Take notes of what you find most interesting, or what you want to remember.

When you finish a chapter, for example, summarize what you have just read to see how much you remember.

CHAPTER 14: FOUNDATIONS FOR

SUCCESSFUL LEARNING

This chapter aims to teach you the basics of learning to learn. We will look at how to deal with our moods and feelings, deal with our attitude towards learning, offer a self-test and discuss possible solutions to well-known learning problems in various case studies.

The goal of this course is to make you aware of the personal conditions that you need for your work. The course contents are prepared in a simple language so that students and parents can also benefit from this knowledge.

Here is an overview of the topics covered in our basic course on learning to learn. In addition to the lessons, we have specified the processing times so you know how much time you should spend on each lesson.

Total processing time:	about 120 minutes

Get in the mood for learning. Learn in the following lessons what "learning" means and how you can improve your previous skills. The following outline gives you an overview of the particular topics that we want to deal with in this context.

Lessons - Overview: What does learning mean?

compliance	about 20 minutes

Here we show how you can recall your previous experiences.

Attunement to the topic "learning."

Basic knowledge	about 20 minutes

Questions about learning

The transience of knowledge

The elements of knowledge

What does learning mean?

Which type of learner am I?	about 20 minutes

Find out with which senses you learn best:
The four learning types
Which type of learner am I?

practice	about 60 minutes

Apply what you've learned to everyday, practical situations:

Case 1 - Learning Problems

Case 2 - Planning Problems

Case 3 - Test Anxiety

Learning with breaks

What does learning mean?

What does "learning" mean and how can you increase your learning ability? Most people assume that this is about talent, about natural talents, about genetic predispositions given to them or not. But - learning is an ability like any other - you have to acquire it or get along with its previous skills.

Everyone can learn to learn when they realize how to improve. Many people are unaware of their potential.

With patience, motivation, and self-confidence, you can realize your goals. In the following lessons, we want to introduce you to the basics of successful learning and a self-test. This gives you an overview of how to successfully approach the topic of learning to learn or which external influences play a role in learning. With this knowledge, you can realize your first steps to increase your learning ability.

Attunement to learning

What attitude do I have to learn?

Everything we do and think is colored by the mood we are in right now. Most clearly, we notice this when we are in love - then the world is "pink" - or if we are melancholy - then the world is "gray." The mood in which you learn and the attitude with which you learn influences your learning success. For you to learn as much as possible in this course, it is important that you become aware of what attitude you have towards learning and what your mood is.

Some people find learning difficult, they have to make an effort, they do not have the desired success, or they are bored at the thought of having to learn. For others, learning is fun; they broaden their horizons, learn concentrated and attentive, and enjoy their success. The examples describe extremes between which there are a wealth of variations.

By tuning in, you can track down your attitude to learning: sit back and close your eyes. Walk with your thoughts into the past. Imagine concrete situations where learning was important to you. Also, remember exams, seminars, courses, anything you associate with learning.

Listen in and observe your moods. How do you feel when you think about learning? Joyful, eager, stressed, bored? Try to get as much of your thoughts and feelings as possible. Do this exercise for 5-10 minutes - then open your eyes and write down your thoughts.

My learning problems...

Nobody always learns equally well. Sometimes you have a bad day and can hardly concentrate on anything. In exam situations, some people are afraid not to remember everything. There may be topics that make you wonder why you should learn this. Learning can be tedious or boring if you are not interested in the topic. You're only halfway there and happy when you have the whole effort behind you.

If you know such situations, you have the opportunity to recognize your learning difficulties. Those who want to master a problem first have to formulate the problem in concrete terms. If you do not know your problems, you will not find a suitable solution.

Many people make the mistake of generalizing their "learning problem." They think they are too stupid or too lazy or that learning is not fun in itself. If you ask yourself more about what is difficult for you, you may conclude that on some days it is unfocused, connections are poorly remembered, embarrassed by fears or something similar. If you can describe your problem concretely, you have already won half - because, for every concrete problem, there is also a solution! Insoluble are only generalizations that obscure the actual problem.

Close your eyes again and imagine situations in which learning was hard for you. Think about precisely what the problem was. Conduct a dialogue with yourself and wonder what exactly was so difficult about that specific learning situation. Ask more carefully - ask for concrete answers and no general phrasing. When you have finished your dialogue, open your eyes again and write down your findings. Honestly, the closer you can identify and name your problem, the closer you are to the solution.

Joyful learning...

Now realize that learning can be fun too. For example, if you love computer strategy games, you need to make a lot of smarter decisions to win against the computer. Is there a specific topic that interests you burning? Are there particular conditions, such as practical experiments in physics that arouse your curiosity? Are you looking forward to your success and recognition if you have written a good grade? Do you enjoy competing with others, maybe in a card game? Has there ever been an issue that interested you so much that you forgot everything around you? Are there any specific teachers that make learning fun?

Follow these suggestions and close your eyes again. Imagine learning situations where learning was a lot of fun. Remember the circumstances in which you have forgotten everything around you and were fully involved. Imagine these situations as accurately as possible - as if they were happening right now. Feel the joy that you had with it.

Then ask yourself again in the dialogue, what exactly gave you so much pleasure in this situation. Do not settle for the first thought, but ask more closely. The better you understand yourself, what made you fun in these learning situations, the better you understand the source of your strongest motivation. Try to figure out your strengths, because they will be the most powerful tools for your success.

After you have finished the dialogue, open your eyes again. Write down your findings. The more accurately you can describe these situations, the more you will learn about your strengths.

Questions about learning

Does our learning ability have anything to do with age?

"You cannot teach old dogs new tricks."

Who does not know this saying? But does our brainpower decrease as we get older? Granted, our muscular coordination, speed of reaction, and memory decline with age. However, our ability to learn is never lost! We have a wealth of experience that we have accumulated throughout our lives, enabling us to classify and understand complex issues better and faster.

"Nobody is too old to learn."

We can learn as well in old age as we can in youth. Age is not a guarantee for fast learning. The care of the mind and the feelings is comparable to physical training. Those who have been physically active throughout their lives will (usually) be fitter in their old age than those who only start exercising their muscles at the age of 60. But it's never too late to start training.

The more we cultivate our intellect in our lives, develop our emotional life, train our character, the easier we will learn as we age. We have accumulated a wealth of experience that can help us quickly identify new issues. Those who have learned from their experiences can easily compensate for an age-related drop in performance. If someone has learned to approach other people and to communicate with them, they will be more socially active in their old age, receive new suggestions and maintain their mental fitness.

Can we learn too much?

"I always learn!"

No - we can only learn too much at once or too much in too short a time - but we cannot learn too much. The more we learn, the easier we learn. The more we know, the easier it is for us to link new information. The more connecting possibilities we have, the easier it is for us to process further information. If we have thought through and structured the material well, we have no limits - the absorption capacity of the human brain is unlimited.

Are mistakes allowed?

"Without one thing going wrong, you never became a master."

Errors are usually negatively affected - that's already in the word. No one likes to make mistakes - perfection and perfection are the ideals of our society today. This is okay - we are spurred on by it. However, the claim to perfection should not prevent us from trying out new things, from making new experiences and thus from learning opportunities.

Those who are afraid of mistakes should realize that learning is only possible if we "allow" mistakes. Errors show us in which areas we can become even better - we have to learn to handle mistakes constructively. No one does not make mistakes, but some people do not learn from their mistakes.

For example, anyone venturing into a new uncharted territory can not resort to existing knowledge. Who leads a project group for the first time, will not make everything perfect immediately. In such situations, it is important not to sabotage yourself by negative self-criticism, but to observe what was right and to see new learning opportunities in the mistakes. Only those who recognize mistakes can even learn! Seeing your own mistakes is the first step in becoming aware of your potential for development.

Learn alone or in a group?

"What if I had not dealt with smart people and learned from them?"

Piaget once said that we become human only through human beings. By this, he meant that we are induced by other people to recognize our possibilities. We see through others what we cannot, and thereby, others can become our role model - our teacher.

Learning in groups can be more successful and enjoyable than learning alone. Many people have more ideas than a single person, fun together is more excellent, and we can handle the challenges more easily. Learning in groups can increase our social skills, we work in groups not only on the subject but also on our ability to work in a team. In groups, manners and rules must be respected. If we manage to be constructive and fair, not devalue anyone and involve all, learning in groups is successful.

Chapter 15: Making the Connection

Gaining Access

A memory can be recorded unconsciously and stored away for some time, all that is needed is the connection to gain access. Memory is more of an activity than a place. Any given memory is deconstructed and distributed in different parts of the brain. Then, for the memory to be recalled, it gets reconstructed from the individual fragments.When it comes to old memories, they're forgotten, but not gone.

Associative memory is defined as the ability to learn and remember the relationship between unrelated items such as the name of someone we have just met or the aroma of a particular perfume. People with exceptional memory are simply exceptional at making a relation or association to the connection for the memory.

As we talked about in the previous chapter If you can't remember the name of an old classmate, try an association, such as trying to remember the names of other classmates. Similarly, when trying to remember the name of a movie or song, think about the stars of the film or the tune's lyrics, you will suddenly make the connection to whatever you were looking for.

Learn the best memory trick used by professional memory performers. Memory performers have a simple way at getting access by using Visualization and Association.

Visualization is seeing with the mind's eye, it is a muscle that can be grown, strengthened, stretched and flexed.

By visualizing and associating, you convert the boring or abstract information into easy to remember mental pictures.

These images are literally mental hooks that allow you to retrieve the information from your long-term memory.

Relate to Recall

Example: Let's use visualization & association to memorize the shape of the kapok tree, so we can both easily recognize them and remember what they are called.

The kapok tree is found in the rainforest. A giant in the rainforests, the kapok tree can reach up to 200 feet in height.

Due to its extreme height, the kapok towers over the other rainforest vegetation.

For this example, we want to remember the kapok tree and all the other characteristics. But how can we easily memorize that "kapok tree" is what they are called?

The trick is to convert the sound of the word "kapok" to a mental image, then connect that mental image with a mental image of the large tree standing tall in the rainforest, a thick tree that grows above the vegetation in the rainforest.

"Kapok" may sound a bit like "hockey puck" (like pok and puck). It's not necessary to match the entire sound of the word exactly.

Remember, we are just hoping to create a mental hook that we can use to retrieve the fact from memory later. Basically, we're creating an artificial reminder that will jog our memory later. You can now envision hockey pucks hanging from the tall kapok tree.

You can see that the image doesn't need to be complicated. But it does need to be clear about what is being represented.

The more clearly you can visualize the image, the better the image will act as a "hook" for you to retrieve the information from your memory.

That's it! The next time I want to remember one tree from the rainforest, my mind will immediately recall this image of a tree standing tall in the rain forest with hockey pucks being hung from it.

Easy   Ways   to   Remember
The larger, more incredible, sillier, or more outrageous you make the images, the better they will work as mental hooks. Your mind remembers the unusual far better   than   the   ordinary.

Let's try now to remember my mother-in-laws (Sandra) birthday on February 11th, 1975. You would start by associating Sandra

to   the   month   of
February

and the 11th day which is really the most important to remember. Sandra can remind you of sandy and February can make you think of valentines day. So now envision a valentines date on the beach with lots of sand with number 11 made of sand   on   the   beach. There are no limits to how you can use the association hooks. Think about other birthdays you have remembered and try to find the associations you have made to easily remember those dates, you most likely did this without trying or thinking about it. For now on make an effort to be exceptionally good at remembering everyone's birthday.

Use what you already know and have strong images of it to create instant hooks. For example: if someone you have just met has a birthday on May 5th. You already know some friends and family members that have their birthday in May as well. You can put that new birthday and associate that new birthday with all the others in May. Now for the 5th day of the month, you may relate the number 5 to reggie bush when he played for USC. Everyone has different interests and different ways to create hooks the key is to use what you already know to create the strongest image possible.

Memory and Your Senses

Did you know that the impressions received from your five senses of hearing, sight, smell, and taste have a significant role in the retention of information in your mind? These are called **Memory of Sense Impressions**; you'll find that the majority of such impressions are those acquired through the two respective senses: sight and hearing.

The more impressions that you can make regarding an event in time the greater the chances of easily remembering that event. Likewise, it is very important to attach an impression of a weaker sense, to that of a stronger one, in order for that may be memorized. For instance, if you have a good eye memory, but a poor ear memory, it is suggested to connect your sound impressions to the sight impressions. And if you have a poor eye memory but a good ear memory, it is important to link your sight impressions to your sound impressions. In this way, you take advantage of the law of association.

We all know the power of an old song to trigger vivid memories that seem to transport us back in time and space. What songs bring back emotional memories from your past? The songs we love become woven into a neural tapestry entwined with the people, seasons, and locations throughout our lifespan.

Chapter16: Clear your Head

Having a full, stressed head is sometimes so difficult. Having a busy mind can cause you to stress, affecting your mood, learning abilities, physical health, mental health, and much more. When you're brain scattered and you do not know what to focus on—what's more important—you begin to notice that your performance at work, school, and/or home begin to go down, and it's like you can't do anything anymore.

You can find ways to distract yourself through learning, reading, and writing, but before we get into the many ways that learning can clear your mind, let's talk about how we can clear your mind daily, and help get rid of that clutter that has infested your brain!

The first thing that you should do if you are feeling overwhelmed is to talk to someone. Whether it is your best friend, a stranger on some sort of hotline, or even a therapist, having someone to talk to has always proven to help you de-stress and get things off your chest.

Sometimes, holding things in can cause even more stress than you began with, pushing you to a breaking point that could end badly. When this happens, you are simply causing your own stress. This could all be avoided if you would just talk to someone.

Keeping a diary has also helped many people! When you have a journal or diary to write your feelings down in, it feels as though your feelings are leaving your body through your hand and into the paper. Many people write in diaries religiously, using them daily. These people that write daily have books upon books to show their dedication to writing their thoughts and feelings down. Why don't you just give it a shot?

You can also help de-stress by distracting yourself. When you have something to do all day, you won't have time to dwell on things that have happened, things that might happen, and things that will happen. Thinking about your problems is just a waste of time; time that you could be spending de-stressing and relaxing before you find a way to solve the problems that you are experiencing.

Exercising is one of the best stress relievers. When you put all of your anger and frustrations into a punching bag, it is as if you can feel the stress levels going down with each punch and kick. Everything that you do at the gym usually has a purpose. When you go for a run, it is usually to think or to relax. Strength training and kickboxing are often used to get your anger out. There is an exercise for everything; I swear.

Going for long slow walks in a calming environment is also something that you should think about doing. I recommend finding a lake or pond somewhere near you and going for a nice long walk by the water. The sounds of nature have been proven to calm a lot of people. Some people even find it useful for when they are having trouble sleeping.

Speaking of sleep; stress and mind clutter can also be caused by sleep deprivation. It is so important to get and efficient amount of sleep for so many reasons! I cannot say that enough, people! Sleep is so important for your mood, learning abilities, and your energy. Without sleep, you are almost destined to be stressed, tired, and cranky!

I know I've already mentioned meditation in two chapters already, but this is another thing that you could do to clear your mind and de-stress. When you meditate, as I've said before, the main goal is to find peace and forget what is going on in your busy life for a moment. All you have to do is find somewhere comfortable to sit, close your eyes and focus on your breathing or heart beat. Just give it a shot and see how it goes.

When you find that you are in need of a distraction due to the clutter that has fogged your brain, some work may be all that you need!

Some people say that reading a book is all it takes to distract them from their everyday life as they are transported to a world where there are no stresses for them to worry about. In the land of

Winterfell, you aren't the one is getting ready for battle. When you are transported to Saint Vladimir's school for vampires, you don't have to worry about who's going to find out your secret. You get to watch other people deal with stresses that are far worse than yours.

Sometimes reading is not only an escape, but it could also be a reality check; even when you're reading fiction. You often realize that the problems that you are face could be worse; even if the problems that you are reading are fictional. It is important to realize that whatever problem you are facing, someone out there probably has it worse. It also gives you a chance to try out your speed reading skills!

You may also find that some of the techniques that we mentioned in earlier chapters can help you with finding a calmer place. This could include sitting down with a jigsaw puzzle. Puzzles increase concentration, taking your mind elsewhere and allowing you to bring your thoughts to something more serene and calm.

Doing a crossword puzzle might even be a good idea! Really when it comes to de-stressing, anything that you do that can take your mind off the hustle and bustle of your everyday life is something that you should try!

It always comes down to your personal preferences, what is going on in your life, and why you feel the need to de-stress. You may need a distraction from a certain friend or your parents. This would mean going somewhere that you may not

Chapter 17: Active Learning

A lot of learning is passive. Students sit in a classroom and listen to a teacher or professor give a lecture. The only stimulation they get is auditory as they take in the words that the professor says. They may occasionally get some visual stimulation, but they don't actually participate in the process.

Passive learning is simply not as effective as active learning. When students take an active role, they learn and retain information easily.

What is Active Learning?

Active learning involves giving students the opportunity to get involved with the material they are learning. In addition to listening to an instructor, they engage with the material through reading, writing, asking questions, discussing what they have learned, and on new material.

It may be helpful to think of the way we learn vocabulary as an example. A teacher can stand at the front of the classroom and explain a new word to you by writing it on the board and defining it. However, the students who are most likely to retain the word and make it part of their vocabulary are those who use it in conversation and think about it.

Benefits of Active Learning

Now let's talk about the benefits of active learning. Here they are:

Active learning helps move information from short-term to long-term memory because you have to use what you learn in multiple ways.

By using multiple kinds of learning (verbal, visual, auditory, etc.) active learning increases the chances that you will absorb information since we all have different learning capabilities.

Active learning can help you learn how to learn by revealing the techniques and tips that are most likely to help you excel in the classroom.

Active learning promotes problem-solving skills and improves critical thinking by making students engage with what they learn.

Students who use active learning are more enthusiastic about learning than students who learn in a passive environment.

As you can see, there are many significant benefits to active learning.

How to Make Active Learning Part of Your Routine

Teachers may use active learning as a technique, but even if your teachers don't, you can use it in your personal study time. This is another area where it may be helpful to study with a partner or team.

You can talk about concepts, share information and insights, and use the time you spend together to understand what you have learned.

Even if you study alone, you can incorporate active learning into what you do. For example, you might:

☐ Make flashcards, which incorporates writing, and then read them out loud to add speaking and listening into the mix.

☐ Draw pictures or watch videos related to the subject you are studying.

☐ Seek out real world examples of what you have learned and think about them critically.

☐ Take time to reflect on what you have learned and put it into context in terms of other things you know.

These techniques can help you retain what you learn and make studying an activity that you look forward to.

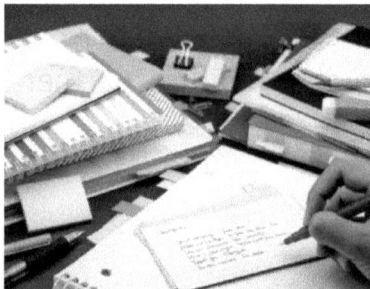

Of course, active learning is not the only accelerated learning technique you can use. In the next chapter, I'll share several other techniques that you may find beneficial as you pursue your studies.

Chapter 18: One Step Ahead: How to

Start Learning Before You Learn

Once you have gone through the lists of do's and don'ts, and you have adjusted your lifestyle to accommodate your newfound accelerated learning, it is time for you to take the next step in this process, and begin what you have been wanting to do this entire time – it's time to take the first step in learning how to learn faster than ever before, and learning how to retain that knowledge.

So, let's begin with a situation you may find yourself in, and I will show you how to use accelerated learning to get the most out of the situation, without you having to stress about it or cram for performance.

Let's say that you are in high school, or college, or that you are in the running for a job promotion at work. Your teacher (professor, or boss) walk up to you with a thick book and tell you that you need to read it that night, and that you are going to be expected to show what you have learned from it in the morning.

For most people, they will then take the book, dutifully go home, get through a quick dinner and nightly routine, then they will settle in with the book and begin reading through each page, one word at a time.

Now, you might be thinking, how else are they supposed to learn? How are they going to show that they have done the assignment when they return to school (or work) the next day? How are they going to show that they are able to advance?

Though it might seem like a hopeless cause, there is actually something you can do that will save you both a lot of time and energy.

In order to effectively make the best use of your time, you are going to have to learn a trick that will make this endeavor a lot easier – learn how to read, understand, and address the assignment, and just the assignment.

That's right. Many people end up working overtime and reaching into overkill as they attempt to learn new material. Sure, it is important to have a full understanding of what you are supposed to know, but what you are supposed to know and what you think you are supposed to know are two very different things.

Let's back up a few steps, and give you an idea of what I am talking about.

First, let's consider a college student who has been given a thick book and an assignment they need to fill out. They could sit down and go with the old fashioned method of reading through the entire book, then stumbling through the questions on the assignment, trying to remember what they were supposed to learn in the first place – a method that proves to be only more frustrating as they have to go back and look up the answers they missed in the first place.

Or,

They could approach the assignment from a different angle, and not only save themselves a lot of time and energy, but also ensure that they are going to get the best results possible on the assignment.

To do this, you are going to shift your focus from looking at the project first, then the assignment, to looking at the assignment first, then shifting to the project.

Let me clarify. Instead of reading the entire reading material that you were given to read in a single evening, you are going to look over your assignment, you are going to learn what you need to know from the book, then you are going to read over the pages of the book until you are able to effectively answer the questions that are on your assignment.

Perhaps you are supposed to answer questions about a specific scenario, character, or experiment. Does this mean that you have to read the entire thing word for word in order to get these answers? Of course not! Instead, skim the pages with a purpose. Don't look for the fine details, look for the answers to your question.

As you come across the answers you are looking for, record them on the assignment (or wherever you are supposed to record them) and move on to the next. There is no need to get bogged down with all the fine details of something that in the end really doesn't matter. So don't do it.

Your brain is dealing with tons of information all day, every day, and it naturally selects what is important and should be remembered, and the information that is useless for the long term, and is best to be forgotten.

Though you can't always do this as smoothly as your brain will naturally, you can train your brain to read over material looking for the answers that you have in front of you on your assignment. Answer the questions (or obtain the information your employer wanted you to obtain) and be done with it.

Another interesting thing to note is that when you are reading like this, your brain is more likely to hold onto the information long–term naturally, as it isn't being bombarded with information that it deems to be useless in the long run.

And one final thought before moving on to the next chapter:

Remember practice makes perfect. You may have difficulties with this at first, but if you give it time, and you diligently practice this technique, you will find that it soon comes as second nature to you, regardless of where you are or what you are reading.

Chapter 19: LEARNING - ONLY WHERE

BEST?

A Type Question: Learning at home or in the library?

First, find out where to study: library (here are some college libraries), at home, or a combination of both.

The one is so distracted by his living environment (telephone, refrigerator, household, roommate ...) that he prefers to go to the library, the other would like to leave his materials to be able to get back in the next day and therefore draws his own Desk in front. Everyone has to make that decision on their own. There is no right or wrong here.

If you are unsure, you should try it out. Often there are alternatives to the university library in the city, public book clubs, archives, jobs in museums.

We will now focus on the workplace at home, as it has the most design options here.

2. Separate workplace and relaxation area strictly!

First of all, it is important to have a stable job. And use this place just for learning. Not to eat, to read newspapers, to watch TV, etc. In return you should not use the "relaxation zone" to work (eg the favorite chair where you always read the good book today to learn). The classic learning place is the desk.

But there are also people who are much better on the floor (eg on a special carpet, cloth), the bed (here can help to distinguish a "learning day blanket"), an extra table in the kitchen or ... learn.

If a strict separation is not possible, you can manage with tricks and rituals. For example, if you only have one table that serves as a desk, dining table, coffee table, etc., you can change the position and place a tablecloth to eat. Other rituals include putting the teddy bear on the desk, putting on a "learning T-shirt", using a specific pen ...

Again, it is important that these rituals are then used exclusively for learning!

Attention should be paid to the conscious distinction. After some training time, the "workplace" is linked to "learning". And starting is much easier. In a sense, the brain is "working" as the employee goes to work tomorrow morning. Learning becomes a matter of course.

3. What belongs to the workplace, what not?

The workplace itself should be adapted to the needs of its external design. For example, one person only needs one book, a pen and a piece of paper, while the other makes markings in different colors, pastes notes, learns from three books at a time, or paints what he has read on large sheets on the wall.

All necessary aids should be prepared before starting work. This avoids foraging often used as an escape route. Things that distract from learning and interfere with concentration have lost nothing in the workplace.

So it is helpful to banish the TV, to clear the remote control, turn off computer, cut off Internet connections, the phone, mobile phone to silence ...

If you work at a desk, you should have enough space to spread (at least 100x60 cm). The height depends on the height. and use a comfortable height-adjustable swivel chair that allows frequent position changes.

4. The right environment for the workplace - climate, noise, temperature, light

So important is a good working atmosphere. Here it helps to hang a sign on the door, so you will not be disturbed and all sources of interference such as telephone, mobile phone, doorbell, etc. to silence. If you still feel disturbed, for example by the classmates in the library, the fridge, the birds, ear plugs will help (pharmacy!).

Even a good working temperature can significantly affect your well-being. If you can learn well at 25 ° C, you should become a tropical expert. All others are recommended to find out their own learning temperature. Generally, the warmer, the more tired you become. On the other hand, keeping one's cold feet off concentrated learning, for example. An optimum can therefore be: heating down, learning at 18 ° C and put your feet on a hot water bottle. If the feet are warm, the rest of the body will rarely freeze.

Also important is good ventilation. So you should ventilate at regular intervals (eg breaks) or go to the fresh air. Lack of oxygen also has a negative effect on the concentration.

Those who learn a lot need good light for this. The 40-watt bulb (Watt in terms of the light intensity of a now no longer available light bulb, equivalent to about 400 lumens) is usually not enough. Ideal are: halogen lights or LED lamps with about 600 lumens, desk at the window (if not too much distraction comes from outside!), Multiple light sources ... also here, according to your own needs! Energy-saving lamps should only be used if you like the light - some do not get along well with it.

5. The perfect workplace for learning - tips at a glance

Here again the most important points that should be clarified at the learning place:

Correct lighting

Ordinary ventilation

Right temperature

Well equipped desk

Separation of work and relaxation area

Chapter 20: Conceptual Clarity

More or less, conceptual clarity implies the ability to comprehend the idea, comprehend the explanation behind its reality, comprehend the procedures in question, to a degree that one can make it straightforward enough for the normal man to identify with it in basic terms.

6.1 Clearly Understanding the Subject Topic

During the most recent four decades, researchers have occupied with investigating that has expanded our comprehension of human cognizance, giving more prominent knowledge into how information is sorted out, how experience shapes seeing, how individuals screen their own seeing, how students contrast from each other, and how individuals get the skill. From this developing group of research, researchers and others have had the option to integrate various fundamental standards of human learning. This developing comprehension of how individuals learn can possibly impact altogether the idea of training and its results.

SEVEN PRINCIPLES OF HUMAN LEARNING

1. Learning with comprehension is encouraged when new and existing information is organized around the significant ideas and standards of the order.

2. Learners use what they definitely know to build new understandings.

3. Learning is encouraged using metacognitive methodologies that distinguish, screen, and manage subjective procedures.

4. Learners have various procedures, approaches, examples of capacities, and learning styles that are a component of the collaboration between their heredity and their related involvements.

5. Learners' inspiration to learn and feeling of self-influences what is found out, what amount is found out, and how much exertion will be placed into the learning procedure.

6. The practices and exercises in which individuals connect with while realizing shape what is found out.
 7. Learning is improved through socially upheld connections.

Take care of issues in that space, however, realizing many disengaged certainties isn't sufficient. Research obviously shows that specialists' substance information is organized around the major sorting out standards and center ideas of the space, the "enormous thoughts" (e.g., Newton's second law of motion in material science, the idea of advancement in science, and the idea of farthest point in arithmetic) (see, for instance, Chi et al., 1981; Kozma and Russell, 1997). These enormous thoughts loan lucidness to specialists' huge information base; assist them with observing the profound structure of issues; and, on that premise, perceive likenesses with recently experienced issues. Research additionally shows that specialists' techniques for deduction and tackling issues are firmly connected to rich, efficient groups of information about the topic. Their insight is associated and composed, and it is "conditionalized" to indicate the setting wherein it is pertinent. In the event that one thinks about cutting edge study as pushing understudies along a continuum toward more prominent skill, at that point propelled study ought to have as its objective encouraging understudies' capacities to perceive and structure their developing assortment of substance information as per the most significant standards of the control. In this way, educational plan and guidance in cutting edge study ought to be intended to create in students the capacity to see past the surface highlights of any issue to the more profound, increasingly key standards of the control.

Educational plans that underscore expansiveness of inclusion and straightforward review of certainties may ruin understudies' capacities to compose information successfully in light of the fact that they don't get the hang of anything inside and out and accordingly are not ready to structure what they are realizing around the major arranging standards and center ideas of the control. Indeed, even understudies who like to look for comprehension are regularly constrained into repetition learning by the amount of data they are approached to retain.

6.2 Three Bricks of Conceptual Clarity

The present world is portrayed by a move – to be specific, digitalization. In addition to the fact that digitalization generates new developments, innovation, and patterns, it can likewise be seen at all levels: in the assembling business just as in the administration part, both in the private and open divisions. With its new advancements, digitalization is changing our correspondence and collaboration, prompting huge developments in both expert and private life and changing the manner in which we discuss and participate.

Obviously, this pattern is likewise clear in the business division, where whole plans of action are being adjusted or totally reestablished to react to computerized change. This additionally incorporates the idea of New Work. The point here is to make work progressively productive and current so as to advance procedures inside the organization. Notwithstanding strong ideas and another corporate culture, this requires a decent specialized foundation and devices for a profitable coordinated effort. Executing this new approach with every one of its features in a significant manner and bringing it into the organization requires an acquaintance with the three mainstays of the idea: With the blocks, bytes, and practices of new working.

Blocks – Spaces of working

The main B represents Bricks and takes a gander at the physical zone of work, for example, the work environment of every individual worker. This must be adjusted to the requirements of the individual who works there so as to guarantee ideal and productive working conditions. All things considered, structure additionally impacts execution.

For a keen, suitable structure, it is basic to get through customary, immovably characterized office and room ideas and to orientate oneself as indicated by what bodes well for the present work – both as far as space and association: "Reexamine the workplace" is the adage here! The center of feasible work is the adaptable structure of the work environment in purported blocks, adjusted to the individual exercises of the representatives. Here, we have to consider the four Cs depicting the sorts of rooms required: Contemplate, Communicate, Collaborate, Concentrate – spaces for reflection, connection, coordinated effort, and centered movement. There is never again a work area (where everything business-related is done), an espresso kitchen, and a gathering room – rather, there are adaptable rooms that can be utilized diversely relying upon current needs. Notwithstanding person

working environments, there are rest regions, group workplaces, and social gathering focuses on parlor zones and espresso corners for advancing the unconstrained trade of thoughts and information between associates. Also, the idea of the home office is turning out to be increasingly pertinent, as it empowers representatives to ideally sort out their time and assets.

The necessary innovation

The subsequent zone is Bytes, for example, successful IT arrangements and specialized gear. These zones are viewed as the apparatuses of the better approach for working, in that they empower interlinked and versatile exercises inside and past the company.It isn't sufficient to tidy off the switch and get new equipment for the representatives – at last, mechanical advancements that drive more intelligent working are fundamental for fulfilling the changing needs.

These advancements incorporate cloud arrangements that empower you to recover, alter, and share all your data whenever, anyplace. In blend with segment-based programming arrangements, organizations can make an advanced chronicle that contains all approaching and active archives in digitized structure – which is exceptionally advantageous when telecommuting or out and about. Another key case of the new approach is nearness the executives, which not just improves openness by dealing with the accessibility of every representative, yet additionally causes it conceivable to work more effectively without long holding up times.

It is significant that the new, broadened arrangements are incorporated into existing procedures and work processes, whereby repeating procedures can be carefully mapped and institutionalized all-inclusive. Likewise, all necessary data from along the worth chain can be made accessible in a basic and easy to use way, which adds to inward just as outside interconnectedness of organizations and expands the administration quality.

This likewise makes an upper hand on the grounds that the information incorporated at the specialized level can be utilized in an objective situated and practical way. This is significant, given that information and data have become the most significant result of organizations.

With these alluring new arrangements, it ought not to be overlooked that a buy alone isn't sufficient: the frameworks not just must be set up and adjusted, yet every representative who is to utilize them later on and advantage from them must be prepared in like manner. Without this, even the best new arrangements bring no financial preferred position.

End on Bricks, Bytes, and Behavior

Existing business procedures must be changed if the three mainstays of New Work are considered if the blocks and bytes are actualized at all degrees of the organization and if the related difficulties are acknowledged by every person. Get the chance: Jump onto the train of contemporary work and dispatch yourself and your organization into an enhanced, satisfying future.

6.2.1 Evidence

Proof, comprehensively understood, is anything introduced on the side of an assertion. This help might be solid or powerless. The most grounded sort of proof is what gives direct verification of the reality of an attestation. At the other outrageous is proof that is simply predictable with a declaration, however, doesn't preclude other, opposing affirmations, as in incidental proof.

In law, rules of proof administer the sorts of proof that are permissible in a lawful continuing. Sorts of legitimate proof incorporate declaration, narrative evidence, and physical evidence. The pieces of a lawful case which are not in the discussion are known, when all is said in done, as the "realities of the case." Beyond any realities that are undisputed, a judge or jury is typically entrusted with being a trier of truth for different issues of a case. Proof and rules are utilized to choose inquiries of the actuality that are contested, some of which might be controlled by the legitimate weight of confirmation significant to the case. Proof in specific cases (for example capital wrongdoings) must be more convincing than in different circumstances (for example minor common questions), which definitely influences the quality and amount of proof important to choose a case.

1. Analogical Evidence

While not a sort of proof you'd use in court, this sort of proof can be valuable for expanding validity by drawing parallels when there isn't sufficient data to demonstrate something in a work environment examination. The analogical proof uses an examination of things that are like drawing a relationship.

2. Recounted Evidence

The recounted proof isn't utilized in court, however, it can here and there help in a working environment examination to show signs of improvement image of an issue. The most serious issue with this sort of proof is that it is frequently "filtered out" to exhibit just tales that help a specific end. Think about it with distrust, and in blend with other, progressively solid, sorts of proof

3. Character Evidence

This is a declaration or record that is utilized to help demonstrate that somebody acted with a specific goal in mind dependent on the individual's character. While this can't be utilized to demonstrate that an individual's conduct at a specific time was reliable with their character, it very well may be utilized in some working environment examinations to demonstrate goal, thought process, or opportunity.

4. Incidental Evidence

Otherwise called aberrant proof, this sort of proof is utilized to deduce something dependent on a progression of certainties separate from the reality the contention is attempting to demonstrate. It requires a conclusion of realities from different actualities that can be demonstrated and, while not viewed as solid proof, it very well may be important in a work environment examination, which has an alternate weight of verification than a criminal examination.

5. Definite Evidence

An item or report is viewed as expressive proof when it legitimately exhibits a reality. It's a typical and solid sort of proof. Instances of this sort of proof are photos, video and sound chronicles, diagrams, and so on. In a work environment examination, this could be a sound account of somebody's irritating conduct or a photo of hostile spray painting.

6. Advanced Evidence

Advanced proof can be any kind of computerized document from an electronic source. This incorporates email, instant messages, texts, records and archives removed from hard drives, electronic monetary exchanges, sound documents, video records. Computerized proof can be found on any server or gadget that stores information, including some lesser-referred to sources, for example, home computer game consoles, GPS sports watches and web empowered gadgets utilized in home robotization. The advanced proof is frequently found through a web look through utilizing open-source knowledge (OSINT).

Difficulties of computerized proof

Gathering advanced proof requires a range of abilities not constantly required for physical proof. There are numerous techniques for separating advanced proof from various gadgets and these strategies, just as the gadgets on which proof is put away, change quickly. Specialists need to either develop explicitly specialized mastery or depend on specialists to do the extraction for them.

Protecting advanced proof is likewise testing in light of the fact that, in contrast to physical proof, it very well may be modified or erased remotely. Specialists should have the option to validate the proof, and furthermore give documentation to demonstrate its honesty.

7. Direct Evidence

The most dominant kind of proof, direct proof requires no deduction. The proof alone is the evidence. This could be the declaration of an observer who saw direct an occurrence of inappropriate behavior in the work environment.

8. Narrative Evidence

Most usually viewed as composed types of confirmation, for example, letters or wills, narrative proof can likewise incorporate different kinds of media, for example, pictures, video or sound accounts, and so forth.

9. Exculpatory Evidence

This sort of proof can excuse a litigant in a – normally criminal – case. Examiners and police are required to uncover to the litigant any exculpatory proof they find or hazard having the case expelled.

10. Criminological Evidence

Criminological Evidence is a logical proof, for example, DNA, following proof, fingerprints or ballistics reports, and can give verification to build up an individual's blame or blamelessness. Scientific proof is commonly viewed as solid and dependable proof and closes by indicting lawbreakers, its job in excusing the blameless has been all around archived. The expression "criminological" signifies "for the courts". Its utilization in working environment examinations is commonly restricted to genuine cases that may wind up in court.

11. Gossip Evidence

Gossip proof comprises of explanations made by witnesses who are absent. While gossip proof isn't allowable in court, it tends to be pertinent and significant in a working environment examination where the weight of confirmation is less powerful than in court.

12. Physical Evidence

As would be normal, proof that is as an unmistakable article, for example, a gun, fingerprints, rope purportedly used to choke somebody, or tire throws from a wrongdoing scene, is viewed as physical proof. Physical proof is otherwise called "genuine" or "material" proof. It very well may be introduced in court as a display of a physical item, caught in still or moving pictures, portrayed in content, sound or video or alluded to in records.

13. By all appearances Evidence

Signifying "on its first appearance" this is proof displayed before a preliminary that is sufficient to demonstrate something until it is effectively negated or countered at preliminary. This is likewise called "hypothetical proof".

14.   Measurable   Evidence
 Proof that utilizations numbers (or measurements) to help a position is called factual proof. This kind of proof depends on   research   or   surveys.
 15. Tribute Evidence

One of the most widely recognized types of proof, this is either spoken or composed proof given by an observer having sworn to tell the truth. It tends to be assembled in court, at a statement or through an affirmation.

Chapter 21: Strategies to Affect Memory and Enhance Learning

It has already been made clear that one of the best ways to learn is to actually do or practice whatever it is you are trying to learn. This is because when you practice something, you are repeatedly registering the information, which helps to commit it to long term memory quicker. Numerous studies have shown that there is actually a direct correlation between the amount of practice that is carried out when learning something new, and the likelihood that the information will be remembered.

When considering practicing something, it is important to differentiate between practice, and repetition. Repetition alone cannot, and does not, improve your ability to learn, as repetition is just carrying out an exercise without involving yourself in it mentally. When you practice something, you are invested in it and therefore it registers itself in your memory quicker, and you can recall it more easily.

To demonstrate how different repetition and practice are, two psychologists carried out a test where they asked people to draw the features of one of the most commonly handled coins in the US. These people were guaranteed to have handled the coin thousands of times over a five year period, so you would think that reproducing the details on the coin would have been easy.

However, when the final results were tallied, nearly everyone who took part in the test had failed to recreate the detail on the coin. This was attributed to the fact that while they handled the coin multiple times a year, it was a repetitive action, and the people were not invested in taking in the details of the coin.

Two British psychologists from Cambridge observed the same result when the BBC in was changing its wavelengths. The BBC had been running an ad campaign to announce the change in frequencies for a few months, meaning that the group of people tested should have heard the advert at least a hundred times by the time the study was being carried out. However, when asked to reproduce certain details in the advertisement, once again most people failed, with many of them literally resorting to guess work to try and fill in the details.

There are many other ways you can improve the learning process other than practice. For instance, there are certain things that you will not even have to memorize to learn. Certain sequences and patterns can be recalled accurately as long as the principle involved is understood. For instance, mathematical sequences such as the Fibonacci sequence do not have to be learned if you understand the principle behind them.

Many studies have revealed that when trying to learn something, it is much more effective if you remember the principle behind what you are trying to learn, rather than the specifics. When it comes to accelerated learning, it is therefore much easier to remember the principle rather than the actual information. This is one of the easiest ways for you to amass a large amount of information in the memory with the least amount of effort. It is also easier to trigger a recall of information if you remember the principle behind it.

For instance, the English speakers in an Accelerated Learning German class found it very hard to differentiate the different genders for words in the foreign language. However, after being given a mnemonic exercise that emphasized the principles behind the association of genders, they were able to deduce the different genders of words based on those principles. This ability to deduce the genders of different words in seconds meant that they were able to learn German at an increased pace. Another way to help you remember, and therefore increase the chance that you will learn something quickly is to attach meaning to that thing. In 1975, researchers Craik and Tulving carried out a study to find out how people would remember a set of 60 words. The criteria they used were the visual appearance of the words, the sound of the words, or the meanings of the words.

They found that when it comes to the appearance and sound of the words, people would recall less than 30% of the words presented to them. However, when asked about the meaning of the words, people would recall almost 75% of all the words that they were asked to remember.

In its simplest form, this study showed that unless you attach some sort of meaning to something, and you understand it, then your ability to learn about that thing will drop drastically. Once you have attached meaning to it, then your brain will be able to associate it with other things or pieces of information, making it easier for you to remember. Therefore, if you are not involved in absorbing the information, it will not be processed properly and it will literally 'go in one ear and out the other'.

This also explains why practice and repetition are so important to learning. By practicing and repeating exercises and information, you are attaching meaning to those things, making them easier to recall in the future.

Conclusion

You adapt best in a low-stress condition you can make best your very own learning style • We are in the data age, we went from muscle influence to mind influence • A production line can get old medium-term by a difference in innovation, nonetheless, your mind just changes • "The best riches creation exists between your ears" • Greatest resource is learning capacity • In the 50s, the old worldview normal idea that every individual had: • The Learning years - school and training • The procuring years - the time you worked • The longing years - an opportunity to unwind and retirement • People today will have 5 full professions, 14 all day occupations • All information for current employments are getting out of date at 40% every year • another alumni from a cutting edge University is progressively able to carry out the responsibility of an architect of 30 years since occupations keep on changing at a fast pace • Continue to learn after school, for motivations behind more significant compensation and aggressive edge • "today, it's not possible for anyone to expect all day business, in any case, they can turn out to be everlastingly employable"

• Think of yourself as independently employed, you offer your support of your present boss • You are responsible for advertising, account, preparing, r and d, upkeep of your own help • You are paid for the estimation of your own administrations

• The 7 popular expressions for change in enormous organizations (The Big R's) • Reorganization - to move individuals around so they produce more • Restructuring - cease things clients aren't willing to pay for, moving more prominent assets to spots to get more noteworthy worth that clients are eager to pay for • Reengineering - cutting back, disposing of not helpful or wasteful contributions to get more yields • Reinventing - hoping to perceive what to do on the off chance that they needed to begin once again today, investigating the future to perceive what they need to do to be fruitful later on • Revaluation - checking if this is the genuine business they need to be in • Refocusing - concentrating their time, exercises, and assets so they can do what they are superb at • Regain control - being proactive about their course

• The Big R's ought to be utilized in your very own organization • Look at the R's at regular intervals and they should change

• Fears of instability are at an unsurpassed high due to the adjustment on the planet • The explanation individuals are apprehensive is that they are most exceedingly terrible off, that is the reason the vast majority attempt to ward off change, they feel that they will get unbound

• Gap examination - Where you are currently and where you need to be, make sense of how to fill the hole • "What is keeping me down to arriving at my objective?"

• Experience of self-improvement is perhaps the best inspiration - Harvard University • When individuals quit learning they start to stagnate, acquire dread, be progressively pushed, and will in general be increasingly stressed

1. You can pick up anything you should be what you need to be 2. Figuring out how to learn is the most astute thing to learn, it is the key capacity to make everything else conceivable in your life 3. Everyone can adapt better, quicker, and simpler on the off chance that they make sense of how they learn and how their cerebrum functions 4. Your insight isn't fixed, it is a muscle, you need to practice it 5. To procure more, you have to find out additional, there is no restriction to the amount you can adapt along these lines there is no restriction on the amount you can acquire 6. You can accomplish any objective, take care of any issue by procuring any expertise that is required for that circumstance